Illustrated

TRIUMPH

BUYER'S ★ GUIDE™

Richard Newton

MBI Publishing Company

First published in 1994 by MBI Publishing Company, PO Box 1, 729 Prospect Avenue, Osceola, WI 54020-0001 USA

MBI Publishing Company books are also available at discounts in bulk quantity for industrial or sales-promotional use. For details write to Special Sales Manager at Motorbooks

International Wholesalers & Distributors, 729 Prospect Avenue, PO Box 1, Osceola, WI 54020-0001 USA

Library of Congress Cataloging-in Publication Data
Newton, Richard
   Illustrated Triumph buyer's guide / Richard Newton. — 2nd ed.
      p: cm. — (MBI publishing company illustrated buyer's guide series)
      Includes bibliographical references (p.   ) and index.
      ISBN 0-87938-917-6
      1. Triumph automobile. 2. Automobiles—Purchasing. I. Title. II. Series.
   TL215.T7N48   1994   94-26703
   629.222'2—dc20

On the front cover: Three of the most popular sports cars Triumph ever produced. Clockwise from front; a 1958 TR3A, a 1974 TR6 and a 1977 Spitfire 1500. *David Gooley.*

On the back cover: Built only during 1968, the TR250 was really an interim car between the TR4A and the much-anticipated TR6. *Plain English Archive.*

Printed in the United States of America

Contents

Acknowledgments

The reality of writing a book is that no one does it alone. Especially a book as successful as this one has been. The most helpful people are those who were most critical of the first edition. There's always a certain amount of anguish when people tell you that they don't like your writing style, or remind you that you left out some very important facts. After reflection you come to realize that this criticism is meant to make the next edition even better than the first.

Richard M Langworth and Charles Runyan were two vigorous critics of the earlier edition. I would like to take this opportunity to say that they provided a tremendous amount of help by making some very direct suggestions about how to improve the latest edition. Hopefully this new edition improved as a result of all their suggestions.

I would also like to thank Mike Cook who has always been very supportive of the early editions. Mike Cook deserves a lot of credit not only for the help he provided with this new edition, but for all that he has done for the preservation of Triumphs in general. Even though Mike has spent the last several decades working for Jaguar I know that he wishes that Triumph had continued in the tradition he so fondly remembers. Mike will always be a member of the Triumph faithful.

The most helpful people were those of you who purchased the first edition of the book. Without your help this second edition would not have been possible. I'm very grateful for all the support that's come from each and every reader. You've made this book a tremendous success. With your continued support we can continue the glory that was Triumph.

Investment Ratings

When the first edition of this book was published people actually believed that they could make money buying old cars and restoring them. People invested in old cars the same way that they might dabble in the commodities market.

Today people buy old cars because they enjoy them. The cost of restoration has become so towering that you can only justify the expense on the basis that you enjoy the car. Old cars are for fun. This is the way it was when I began in the hobby, and it's the way it will remain for the foreseeable future.

An important point you should always remember when you buy a Triumph is that the condition of the car is far more important than the particular model. A TR4 in nice condition will be a far better buy than a rusted and worn out TR6. The car you can drive is always better than a car that comes home in boxes.

If you're shopping for a Triumph spend some time going to Triumph shows and club meetings. Attend as many English car shows as your schedule will permit. Remember, you're buying this Triumph to enjoy for several years, if not several decades. A few extra months spent surveying all the Triumphs in the market will pay extra dividends.

The best thing you can do is to join the local Triumph club and ask a lot of questions. The members of the local Triumph club have already driven down the road that you intend to take. Their advice can save you from making the mistakes that they've already made. Spitfire owners know about the current Spitfire prices and TR3 owners know what's a fair price on a given TR3. Asking a lot of questions before you actually purchase a Triumph can make owning one a lot more fun.

★★★★★ These are the best Triumphs. You can expect to pay extra for these cars. They usually have historical significance and are well known. They're often sold between collectors and are seldom advertised. Most of the cars in this category have already been restored or are in original condition.

★★★★ These are excellent cars to purchase. They may be lacking in historical value but they have a tremendous amount of fun value. These are usually Triumphs that have all the traditional values, but are lacking in the technical areas. There will be more than enough work to keep you busy on the weekends. When you own a restored example of one of these cars you have a car that other Triumph owners will admire.

★★★ These are good values. The problem with this type of Triumph is that you can never recover all the money you put into the car. The idea with this type of Triumph is to purchase one that's in very good condition and simply maintain the car. First time Triumph owners usually start with this sort of car. Just be careful that you don't buy one of these cars if you have little time and money.

★★ These are Triumphs that are purchased just for fun. There's very little value in the car except for personal recreation. Then again isn't that what a Triumph is all about anyway?

★ This is the Triumph to avoid. These are usually rolling wrecks. Don't delude yourself that with just a little effort this type of Triumph will be just fine. These are the cars that make people leave the car hobby. Avoid them at all cost.

Introduction

The Essence of a Sports Car

Driving a TR3 down a country lane with the wind pouring over the cut-out door and twisting that oversized steering wheel around the corners is pure pleasure. Then there's that deep Triumph sound coming from the exhaust, which was always a Triumph characteristic, until the wheeze of the TR7 arrived.

Triumph produced some very nice, and some very nasty cars. It pays to spend a little time to figure out which Triumph is going to give you the most pleasure, not in financial terms, but in terms of fun. Working on old British sports cars is an overrated experience. At the same time driving them is seriously underrated.

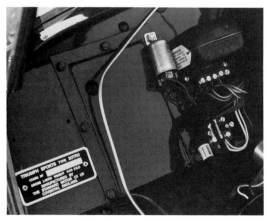

This is the type of detail work you can expect to find on a top quality show car. Notice the little tag on the voltage regulator and the cleanliness of the wires themselves. It is actually nicer than when the car left England. This takes a lot of effort and is what makes certain cars special. *Author collection.*

Your neighbors like Triumphs and your friends like Triumphs. The cars remind them of an era when things were simpler. An era before the government could tell us what sort of car was good for us. Triumphs are the cars of our youth.

You have to like Triumphs for what they are. They're an inexpensive way to enjoy driving. Triumphs are not state of the art high performance cars. They never were, even when they were brand new. Triumph never led the engineering world in totally new developments. Triumphs were designed to sell to the masses, especially the American masses. Sports cars were a way to help the British economy recover after World War II.

When the collector car world went crazy in the 1980s Triumph just kept rolling along. Nobody got rich, and nobody lost a half million dollars, on a Triumph. A lot of people though had a lot of fun driving their Triumphs.

A Triumph has always been fun to drive and it's always been a good buy. With a Triumph we're talking about value. For not very much money you can own one of the true sports cars of the era—any era.

Consistency is the hallmark of Triumph history. While the TR series, especially the TR2 and the TR3, were in a class all by themselves, the cars were actually a continuation of the prewar philosophy. The idea was to make them light, fast, and as effective as any sports car on the road.

Even the Triumph GT6, which with its small displacement six seemed unique, was really similar to the Scorpion built in 1932. Even the final effort of Triumph, the TR8, was in some regards similar to the eight-cylinder Dolomite built in 1935.

Triumph began its history with light, spindly, semi-sporting cars like the 10/20 and you could argue that it finished its history with a light semi-sporting car called the TR7. In between these dubious accomplishments Triumph produced any number of highly competitive low priced two-seaters which achieved steady sales.

Any company that produces cars for sixty years is bound to have produced a number of nice cars. Triumph did just that. It's not difficult to understand why they've become so popular with restorers. There's no such thing as a sophisticated Triumph; that's what makes them so easy for your first restoration project. At the same time there are very few cars that are more fun to drive.

The early prewar examples of Triumph are in a class by themselves. Buying and collecting Razoredge saloons and Mayflowers require a special sort of individual.

These Triumph sedans are very scarce cars. Most people will spend their entire lives without ever seeing one. Even people who own TR series cars pay little attention to them. The Gloria Six for example is defined as a classic by the Classic Car Club of America. It's probably the cheapest car to purchase on that list. If it's a sleeper don't expect it to wake up any time soon.

When the average person talks about Triumphs it's the TR series they're referring to. These are the strong Triumphs. From the first TR2s to the last of the TR6s these are the cars that made great noises and handled well enough that you could scare yourself pretending to be Stirling Moss.

No one ever accused the Triumph of being an exotic car. No one ever thought their Triumph was a Ferrari, or even a Porsche for that matter. People like Triumphs—they don't hold them in awe. This also means that they've always been an affordable sports car. They all rate as a good value because you can have a lot of fun without having to sell the wife and children.

The TR's popularity has less to do with its technical attributes, and its competition record, than with its sheer entertainment value. You don't see a lot of enclosed trailers at a Triumph gathering. You just see people having fun while they drive their Triumphs. A friend who's raced them for over twenty years says that "A Triumph is a Triumph, nothing else." This holds for the good features as well as the bad.

The final Triumph was a disaster—the TR7. A major reason was that Triumph decided to go modern in a very big hurry. Triumph, or rather Leyland, made the classic marketing mistake and forgot who their customers were. When we consider these final Triumphs it may be that the only criterion for collecting one of them will be rarity.

Today's best feature of the TR7 is the price. A TR7 convertible can be a lot of fun for very few

This is when you should get worried. The rust means that you probably have even bigger problems that you can't see. Make sure that your offer reflects the effort it'll take to restore a rusted car. This sort of car can consume money quicker than the federal government. *Author collection.*

dollars. This is the sort of car you can may enjoy on an everyday basis more than a TR2. You don't have to baby a TR7 the way the people do with the early TR series cars. Also, a TR7 is one car you don't have to worry about being stolen. Maybe as time passes we'll learn to appreciate these final Triumphs a little more.

The Triumph Spitfire served as a benchmark as to what a cheap sports car could be. It forced BMC to make some changes in the Spridget line, even though BMC said that they had already designed roll-up windows before the Spitfire was introduced. This is the sort of argument only British car owners could appreciate.

The early Spitfires were evil-handling cars when they reached their limit, but up to that point seemed just the ticket for quick driving. The problem was that they used the same rear axle arrangement as the old VW Beetles, an arrangement that would cause the inboard wheel to fold under the car at the very limit of cornering. Very exciting and very scary. One point to remember though is that you'll probably never drive your Spitfire that fast.

One very important facet of the Spitfire was that it led to the production of the GT6. This was a very nice touring car that would have been a tremendous success had Datsun not introduced the 240Z at about the same time.

The little rubber seals and gaskets can quickly add to your restoration costs. No single item will be expensive but the total will astound you. When a car is as nice as this one don't be afraid to pay a premium price. In the long run it'll be cheaper to own than a basket case Triumph. *Author collection.*

Then we come to one of the great mystery cars—the Stag. This car should have been a tremendous success. Throw in a couple of typical British compromises and the car turned into a major marketing disaster. It also has several major and unique drawbacks that you should consider before buying one as a collector car.

The Stag, though, is catching on with the restoration crowd. Every year you see a few more Stags at the car shows. When they're properly restored they're a nice car. The Stag is a touring car, not a great sports car. The Stag is a pleasant car for Sunday trips. As people come to appreciate them you can expect the price to climb.

Inexpensive is a relative term. When you compare a Triumph to a Ferrari the Triumph is downright cheap. Even Triumph parts look like a good buy, when compared to Mercedes parts. Nonetheless Triumphs can destroy a bank balance as quickly as health care programs can wreck havoc with the national debt. The days of really cheap Triumphs are gone. The five hundred dollar Triumph no longer exists. Even junk brings a respectable price. On the other hand your children will look back on this era as being the time when Triumphs were cheap. It's all relative.

The good part is that the price difference between a nice Triumph and junk has narrowed. There is no longer any excuse for purchasing a cheap, but restorable, car. When you compare what it will cost to restore a rolling wreck and a respectable Triumph the good car is actually less expensive. Quality is always cheaper. Don't ever forget this basic principle when you go Triumph shopping.

The best way to shop is to price the nicest examples of your favorite Triumph. This becomes the base line. Then take the asking price of any other Triumph and add to that figure what it will cost to bring the inferior car to the base line example.

$$\begin{array}{ccc} \text{Driveable} \\ \text{Wreck} \end{array} + \begin{array}{c} \text{Cost of} \\ \text{Restoration} \end{array} = \begin{array}{c} \text{Fully Restored} \\ \text{Car} \end{array}$$

The least expensive Triumph will always be the one with the highest initial purchase price. The one that will actually cost the most will be the "90% complete, easily restored" car.

Anytime the left side of the equation is larger than the right hand side you've got a financial problem. Don't ever buy the "easily restored" car for financial reasons. Buy it because you like it. Buy it because you like working on old cars, but never buy to save money. You can buy most restored Triumphs today for less than the cost of the parts the owner put into the car.

Triumphs will never seriously decline in price, having avoided the speculators of the eighties. On the other hand don't expect them to experience a tremendous increase in value either. The Triumph is a car for enthusiasts, not investors.

Triumphs are usually a first foray into restoration. This is good since the Triumph is a fairly easy car to restore. The very primitive nature of the car that allowed it to be inexpensive in the first place now makes it easier to restore.

The TR series, except for the TR7 and TR8, have the classic body hung over a rather substantial frame. This makes it easy to forge ahead with a standard ground up restoration. There are far fewer problems with these early TRs than you'll encounter on the unit body cars.

The Spitfires are more of a problem since the unit body rusts almost as bad as a Porsche. Restoring a rusted Spitfire is something akin to living at one of Dante's lower levels. Once you locate the major rust areas you just keep probing, and hoping that someday you'll find a solid part. Spitfires can end up costing a lot more to restore than the TR3 and they will never come close to the value of a TR3. Be careful and make sure that you really want a Spitfire before your bank balance is destroyed.

Whether you have a Spitfire or, a TR, parts are readily available. You can get almost everything you need for your restoration project in the United States due to the ability of the Asian world to reproduce just about anything that Triumph originally manufactured.

Since a Triumph is usually a first restoration project I'm going to take a few minutes to discuss the general plan.

Except for the Mayflower, Herald/Spitfire, and the TR7/8, all Triumphs are candidates for the classic body-off restoration. Restoration is a lot easier if you can simply remove the body panels from the frame and chassis. The only problem is that removing parts is so easy that your beloved Triumph may still be in this state several years later. As easy as your Triumph is to take apart it'll be a lot harder to put back together. Even more difficult is to put together correctly.

The Spitfire is more difficult to properly restore than a TR3, which is one reason you see so few restored Spitfires. The only way to really deal with a Spitfire is to remove everything and have the body shell dipped into an acid-type bath. Then you can begin replacing rusted panels.

The irony here is that the cheaper car is going to be more difficult, and more expensive, to properly restore. That's why you see so many Spitfires and GT6s with new paint and a repaired interior. Very few people actually spend the time, and money, to restore one of these cars properly.

A good feature of any Triumph is that the major components are reasonably sized. This is no small matter. First, they take up less space in your garage. This means that you can work around them easily.

Secondly, it's easier to find storage space for a couple of TR3 fenders than a Camaro hood. Remember, this is no weekend project. Your prize Triumph could easily spend several years residing in the family garage, in properly labeled boxes.

There was a time when you had to choose between fiberglass body panels and the original Triumph parts. There's still a lot of fiberglass on the market, especially for the early TRs. The problem is that most of this stuff doesn't fit very well. You can spend much time and effort making these body panels look right. Fiberglass should only be used when you can't locate the proper sheet metal.

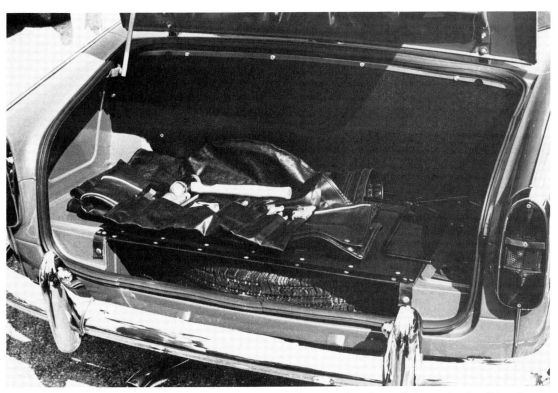

If you're looking at a Triumph with a complete tool kit you're looking at a car somebody cared about. This is the sort of car that brings a premium price on the market.

This type of car is usually known by other Triumph owners and you can generally get a complete history of the car. *Author collection.*

Before you start buying parts make sure that you attend a couple of Triumph gatherings. Ask people where they buy their parts. Remember, there's no need to make mistakes on a Triumph. A lot of people have restored them before you. Their advice can save you a lot of time and money. Advice is cheap. Collecting advice is a lot cheaper than collecting a bunch of expensive tools and parts.

If you have to make a decision between a sound body and chassis and a sound drivetrain, take the sound body. A TR6 with a bad motor is going to be a lot cheaper to repair than a body that is rusted. Body work is always going to be more expensive than engine repair.

I've never seen five good wire wheels on an old unrestored Triumph. One, and sometimes all five, are in miserable condition. New, or reconditioned, wheels are going to get very expensive. If you're considering a car with wire wheels always take into consideration that they probably aren't round, and they're going to add a major item to your budget. A bad set of wire wheels can add hundreds of dollars to the cost of a restoration.

You can simply avoid the headache of wire wheels and do what Triumph did with the TR6, start with alloy, or steel wheels. TR3s and TR4s actually look rather nice with Minilite, or the Minilite look-alikes manufactured by Panasport.

While you're down on your hands and knees checking wheels, also check the condition of the

You're looking at a tremendous amount of work here. Just getting wire wheels to look this good is a major undertaking. Keeping them this way means constant attention, or not driving the car. *Author collection.*

rear shock absorbers. On the TR series, and some of the earlier cars, these were the old lever style shocks, which are expensive to replace. Rebuilt units are available, but they're not particularly cheap. All of these old lever shocks leak, but if they look particularly oil soaked figure the price of new or rebuilt lever shocks into the cost of the car.

While you're still under the car check the condition of the shock links. These are a lot cheaper to replace than the shocks. They're generally in pretty bad shape. Rear shock links are one item that everybody just seems to ignore. It's a shame to ignore them though, since bad shock links can really hurt the ride of a Triumph.

The front shocks are usually worn out on all Triumphs. If you want to replace them, and you probably will, you should seriously consider a set of Koni brand shocks. These are some of the most expensive shocks on the market, but worth the price. If you have a tight budget consider Spax shocks.

The most important thing is that you make a very careful assessment of any Triumph you're considering purchasing. If you look at less than a half-dozen cars before you make your purchase you're asking for trouble.

The problem is not that you'll pay too much initially. The real financial danger is that you're going to spend way too much money getting your Triumph into the condition that will keep you, and your family, happy.

Stop thinking about initial price and pay attention to the condition of the car. In real estate they talk about location being important but with Triumphs it's Condition, Condition, and Condition.

Taking Care of Your New Prize

Assuming that your quest for the Triumph of your dreams is over and the new prize is secure in your garage, what comes next? If you towed your Triumph home, or worse yet, it came home in boxes, you're on your own. Buying a Triumph basket case makes you either a genius, or a major fool. You'll only know the correct answer several years, and several thousands of dollars later.

After your neighbors get through with all their questions. and have stopped asking, "You paid how much?", you'll be ready to attack the car.

First, avoid taking anything apart. This is rule one, rule two, and rule three. Never begin your relationship with your Triumph by removing parts. You need to give your relationship time to develop.

The first thing to do is simply change the oil. Avoid all the latest synthetic oils. They leak in normal cars, imagine how much synthetic oil will leak onto your garage floor from a Triumph.

This is the kind of Triumph to avoid. These are the cars that are offered to you for just a few hundred dollars. They'll end up costing you thousands more to restore than they'll ever be worth. The worst part is that they can really depress you when you finally start to rebuild the car. Begin your Triumph adventure with a car that you're able to drive. *Author collection.*

Use oil from a major oil supplier and you should have no problems. Don't bother looking for a non-detergent oil, that's an old tale that's been passed around the hobby for far too long. I like 10W-30 in any car, and have never had a problem. If you still believe in the old-fashioned non-detergent oil try a single weight type, it can't do any harm.

The next step is to grease all the fittings. Make sure that you have a copy of the manual with you when you start. Some of the grease fittings probably haven't been used in several years, or decades. Take your time and look around while you're doing this. You could learn a lot about your new toy.

You can follow this up next week by flushing the cooling system. Use a very mild flushing agent and follow the directions carefully. Keep flushing the cooling system until clear water comes out of the radiator. It may take several flushes to get the system really clean. Sometimes you have to flush the system on consecutive weekends to really have a clean cooling system. When you're done fill the system with a mixture of anti-freeze and water.

If you think any of the hoses in the cooling system need replacement do it at this time. The longer you put this off the greater the chances are that a hose will break a long way from home. You certainly won't be able to find the correct hose when it does happen. To properly take care of the cooling system you should also replace the thermostat and radiator cap. Plan on one whole weekend to do this job and try to use correct parts. NAPA hose clamps have never looked right on a TR2.

Now that you've built up your confidence let's spend another weekend on the brake system.

There are a couple of items here. First, check the condition of the brake pads and the thickness of the brake rotors. Also look at the rubber hoses and make sure that you don't have any cracks and rips in the rubber.

Next, we're going to flush all the dirty brake fluid out of the system and replace it with new clean brake fluid. This probably hasn't been done in the last decade. You should do it every year. It's a small job that will save you from a lot of brake system problems.

Place your Triumph on four jack stands and check to make sure that you can loosen all the bleeder screws. If you find one or more of them rusted in place, go back in the house and start looking at Triumph parts catalogs.

Assuming that you got all four of them loose, go ahead and suck most of the old brake fluid out of the master cylinder with a turkey baster. Fill the master cylinder with fresh Castrol brake fluid. Now have a friend, or relative, push down on the brake pedal while you open the bleeder screw on the rear wheel cylinder furthest from the master cylinder. Keep bleeding all the brakes until clean fresh brake fluid runs out of the bleeder. Make sure that you keep the master cylinder filled with new Castrol fluid while you do this. If you run the master cylinder dry you just made the job twice as long as it needed to be.

Avoid silicone fluid at this time. You should never mix silicone fluid with conventional fluid. Silicone fluid is wonderful and you should use it in any collector car. The time to install it is when you do a major, and complete, brake overhaul. Changing to silicone brake fluid is a winter project.

The next two items to attend to are the transmission and rear axle oil. This is another weekend project and you're on your own here. You should have enough confidence, and a grease stained manual, by this time to start in on the advanced items.

The idea is to take care of one item at a time. Don't get carried away with major projects during your first year of ownership. All it will do is frustrate you and create havoc with the family budget.

When your Triumph becomes "That car in the garage" you know you're in trouble.

The one item we've neglected is the electrical system in the Triumph. The Lucas electrical system wasn't the greatest to start with. The last five owners only made it worse.

Get a wiring diagram for your Triumph and a test light. Learn to take your time and thoroughly check any electrical problem. Compared to a modern Jaguar the electrical system is very simple. All of the original wire ends and bullet terminals are available from various parts suppliers. This is a big help.

After you get through with all your initial forays into the inner workings of your new Triumph you'll probably know more about the car than the last three owners combined. You'll have a good idea about how to keep it running and you'll also get an idea about where you're going to be spending money in the coming year.

As you work on your Triumph you should always replace broken parts with original Triumph parts. Over the years the previous owners have probably made a lot of changes. Before you try to do anything, make an effort to ascertain if you're working on something original, or whether someone has made an attempt to improve on Standard-Triumph engineering. Always strive to bring the car closer to way it was when it left the Triumph factory. You'll enhance the value of the car, not to mention save yourself some money over the next couple of years.

Before you even get close to purchasing a Triumph though, you should join your local Triumph club. These people can help you. But first you have to ask for the help.

Over the last several years I've had the opportunity to work with a lot of different marque clubs, and in my opinion few groups have the enthusiasm of the Triumph people. They enjoy Triumphs and they even seem to understand them—something that's not always easy. Anyone who owns a Triumph and doesn't belong to at least one of the clubs is missing the chance to learn a lot about how to live with their Triumph.

Chapter 1

Prewar Triumphs

<table>
<tr><td>★★</td><td>Gloria Six,
Dolomite Straight Eight,
Dolomite Two Liter
Super Seven,
Gloria Four</td></tr>
</table>

Early Models

Though Triumph began building cars in 1923, examples from the twenties are virtually nonexistent. With one known exception they're all in England, and likely to remain there. It is superfluous to discuss them here, though they should be noted for the record: the 10/20 (1923-26), 13/35 (1924-26), and Fifteen (1926-30).

The Super Seven, which actually began production in 1927, was offered through 1932. Available in a wide variety of body styles, it was powered by a straightforward, cast-iron three-bearing engine with full-pressure lubrication and a conventional ladder chassis. It was the first significant car in Triumph history, and can be credited with helping establish the marque's reputation.

A fine performer for its size, the Seven accomplished notable feats on endurance runs. Despite a miniscule engine and 21hp, Sevens regularly lapped Brooklands at over 75mph. But the Car's great venue was the rally circuit. None other than Donald Healey, Triumph's leading competitions manager in those days, drove Super Sevens to many high finishes. Such feats attracted a wide audience, and the Super Seven was the highest-volume model during prewar years. Triumph built over 17,000 Super Sevens, counting the derivative Super Eight (which lasted until 1934).

Although plentiful in their day, Sevens and Eights are uncommon on the current collector car markets in the US and England. Those that wend their way across the pond tend to be open models, which is to the good. The pretty little boat-tail roadsters are especially desirable.

What does the Super Seven offer the car collector? Essentially a better-finished, better-performing version of an Austin Chummy. And don't laugh; the Austin Seven is one of the most popular

collector cars in the world. Super Sevens do present difficulty with regard to parts, but the bodies were so simple and functional that repair and even reproduction is not difficult. In no sense, however, should they be considered in terms of a restoration project. This is one case where it pays to buy only the well-restored "gem." Membership in the Pre-1940 Triumph Owners Club is not only a good idea, but essential.

During 1930-33, Triumph produced a succession of automobiles which have not survived in great numbers. None were very interesting to the new-car buyers of those years, nor are they to today's collectors. Most underwhelming among these was the six-cylinder Scorpion, conceptual forebear of the Herald/Spitfire.

The idea of a smooth-running, six-cylinder mini-car was certainly reasonable on paper; but the product, in fact, was a nasty piece of work. The added engine weight (it was derived from the Super Seven) made the Scorpion handle poorly, and it soon acquired a reputation for skittishness which it never lived down. The derivative Twelve/Six was no more successful, and these sixes vanished after 1933.

More important was the Super Nine, direct predecessor to the first Triumph sports cars and worth a place in history for that reason. Conceived out of Managing Director Claude Holbrook's quest for sporting machinery, the Nine had Triumph's first inlet-over-exhaust engine, supplied by Coventry-Climax. It was also the first Triumph to benefit from the hand of a body designer—Frank Warner, one of the most brilliant in his profession.

Soon offered on the Super Nine chassis was the Southern Cross sports model, a high-bodied aluminum roadster probably designed by Ratcliffe of London. The Southern Cross was built by

Salmons & Sons in Newport Pagnell, present home of Aston Martin Lagonda. At about $1,300, this handsome roadster came standard with a big, four-spoke sprung steering wheel, a folding one-piece windscreen with twin electric wipers, carpeting, chrome-plated stone guard, and full instrumentation including rev counter. With only about a liter it was not a screamer, but it did handle nimbly. For the first time, Triumph had a real sports car; and had achieved that granitic ruggedness for which the TR was later known. An extension on the theme was the Triumph Ten, with 1100cc and a shade more horsepower, using the same 87in wheelbase. There were also Southern Crosses on Ten chassis.

Historically the pioneer Triumph sports car, the early Southern Cross, was also fun to drive. It was strictly thirties in character, yet up-to-date with four-wheel hydraulic brakes (a Triumph characteristic since the twenties), decent four-speed gearbox, and lively engine. Examples, however, are almost unknown. If one comes up, and you fancy the opportunity to own a particularly historic Triumph, you'd be well advised to make the investment.

The Glorias

On balance the most sensuously beautiful production cars in Triumph history, the Glorias, reigned from 1934 to 1938, and brought dramatic change to the company. Before Gloria, Graham Robson wrote, "Triumph had made a series of very good conventional cars whose merit lay mainly in their quality engineering. . . . After Gloria, Triumph's reputation for high quality and fine engineering was augmented by cars that were handsome and sporting as well."

E.H. Braverstock's immaculately restored 1932 Super Seven pillarless saloon deluxe at a mid-seventies Triumph rally. That's a real "four-door hardtop"; the suicide doors close against each other and there's no B-pillar to stand in the way when they're open. Note the slim radiator shell, characteristic of late-production Sevens. *Richard Langworth collection.*

For this reason and because pricewise it was "for the classes, not the masses," the Classic Car Club of America has cited the Gloria Six as a "classic." Sixes were built from 1934 through 1937, and were always powered by Coventry-Climax engines. In another manifestation of Triumph's constant repetition of themes, the Gloria from 1935 on had a displacement of 1991cc—exactly the same as the TR2 some twenty years later.

The most memorable characteristic of the Triumph Gloria was its beautiful styling, originally by Frank Warner, later modified by Walter Belgrove. Smooth and rakish, it resembled nothing that had gone before, and was comparable to the contemporary (and now highly desirable) Riley, Alvis, and SS.

The Gloria introduced an American concept: a wide range of types on only two basic models. Included were a four-door, four-light saloon; a tuned version of same called the Special; and a two-door, four-seat tourer, with a tuned Speed model—all variants on eight four- or six-cylinder chassis. The tourers had a novel feature: The top of the door, normally parallel with the ground, was hinged and could be folded down, creating "cutaway" doors.

Shortly into the production run Triumph introduced the Gloria Monte Carlo, designed mainly for rally work, in both four- and six-cylinder variants, the latter being rare. The Monte Carlo carried narrower coachwork and twin spare tires mounted at the rear.

The greatest proliferation occurred in 1935, when Triumph offered no fewer than twenty-nine individual models, including eight Cross & Ellis custom-bodied specials (Golfer's and Foursome coupes in two state of tune with both four- and six-cylinders).

Back this year, now on a Gloria chassis, was the Southern Cross, completely altered, with svelte lines off Walter Belgrove's drawing board. Though resembling the Monte Carlo it lacked a rear seat, and its cutaway doors did not have hinged panels. Standard equipment included a quick-release gas cap; big, accurate instruments; a reversing lamp; and, curiously, twin number plates. (The latter were required by some Continental countries.) Both four- and six-cylinder Southern Crosses came only in the tuned (Vitesse) state, and the six managed over 83mph at Brooklands. These were sensational Triumphs, blessed with a slick, half-synchromesh four-speed gearbox, light steering, engine flexibility, and excellent roadholding with the help of Luvax adjustable shocks. They rank among the most desirable prewar Triumphs.

The first Southern Cross was built on the Super Nine and Ten chassis. It was fairly rudimentary, but nevertheless Triumph's first attempt at a sports car. This example with Coventry number plates is from 1932. The trisected Lucas headlamps have often been defaced with sealed-beam conversions; these are the right ones. *Richard Langworth collection.*

The tuned Glorias of 1935 went by the name Gloria-Vitesse. The modifications included a high-lift cam, larger valves, twin carburetors and more horsepower. Vitesse versions of most body styles were available at about $100 more than standard. Offered as a six-cylinder Vitesse only was Belgrove's Flowfree saloon, one of the most interesting prewar cars. It should be noted by collectors, because any one that surfaces stands to be extremely desirable. Only a handful were built, and the existence of survivors is not confirmed at this writing. With the exception of the Flowfree, which didn't sell, a similar lineup was offered again in 1936.

After 1936 the Climax six was dropped and two Triumph engines added: a four and six of 1496 and 1991cc respectively. The latter used the Climax conn rods and pistons. In body design the Vitesses were the same as standard, except for the four-light saloons which were considerably sleeker.

The following is a brief summary of Vitesse production models written by Glyn Jones in *The Vintage Triumph*, March-April 1976:

1934: No Vitesse variants. Speed model tourer and Special saloon had twin carburetors but standard bodies.

1935: Gloria-Vitesse had twin carbs and enhanced performance but otherwise mechanically similar to Gloria. It did encompass three models not available with standard specification: the

15

Comparison views of the 1935 Gloria (top) and Gloria-Vitesse (bottom) saloons. In addition to more power, the saloon model of the Gloria-Vitesse offered sleeker, less bolt-upright styling. Examples are hotly pursued by collectors. *Richard Langworth collection.*

This handsome 1935 Gloria Southern Cross was displayed by British Leyland in the United States during Triumph's fiftieth anniversary celebrations in 1973. It's an almost perfect restoration, except for ugly sealed beams hidden inside the original Lucas headlamp shells. The Gloria Southern Cross is the most common prewar Triumph encountered by U.S. collectors. *Richard Langworth collection.*

Southern Cross roadster and Monte Carlo four-seat tourer, plus the six-cylinder-only Flowfree saloon.

1936: Same as 1935. A fairly reliable, but not universal, rule for 1935-36 is that Vitesses had two large instruments (tach and speedo), while standard dashes carried four smaller instruments in a metal panel on a wooden board.

1937-38: Vitesse (not Gloria-Vitesse) had a round-edge radiator and two large instruments, but normally these were a speedo and a clock. The engine had no provision for rev-counter drive.

The most confusing model, not usually encountered by collectors, is the four-door, six-light saloon. This could be had as a Climax-engine Gloria, a Vitesse 14/60 or a Gloria Fourteen. Its only ready identification was its Vitesse badge.

The Dolomites

The grandest prewar Triumph, indeed the grandest of all, was the straight-eight supercharged Dolomite of 1935. Patterned closely after the Alfa 9C 2300 (apparently with Alfa's blessing), its engine was a masterpiece of design—Alfa-based but smaller in displacement because Donald Healey was aiming at the two-liter racing class. With blower, the engine developed 120hp at 5500rpm and gave the car a top speed of 100-110mph. In its class it was the fastest sports car of the prewar years, quicker than any contemporary Lagonda or Bentley, cars priced much higher. (The price, complete, was about $6,000.)

The Dolomite's dramatic roadster body was designed by Frank Warner. It was a breathtaking assemblage of vee'd radiator, lean and flowing lines, cut-down doors, fore-shortened and rounded tail. Warner designed lovely flowing fenders, but the cars produced had cycle fenders. Though engine and body were straight out of the Alfa book, the rest of the Dolomite was not. Both cars used the almost universal ladder chassis, but they had different gearboxes, back axles, and suspensions. (Triumph used semi-elliptic springs very tightly

17

damped, and the Dolomite rode like a truck according to testers.)

Evidence suggests that the Dolomite chassis was planned to eventually carry a complete line of luxurious Triumphs, including a magnificent sports saloon on a stretched 132in wheelbase. Alas, the car appeared at the nadir of Triumph's existence, with mounting losses due partly to the Depression, partly to heavy competition in the Triumph price class. Holbrook canceled the Dolomite project in April 1935, and only three complete cars were built. One of these was demolished at a grade crossing in Denmark during the 1935 Monte Carlo Rally.

But that is not the end of the story. Recently, Triumph enthusiasts were tipped off that the other two cars had been located in England. Both are now undergoing restoration. And as surely as the sun will rise tomorrow, one or both of these cars will one day be for sale. The price will be the highest ever asked for a Triumph.

Their existence merits their mention in these pages. You may never be able to own a Dolomite Straight Eight, but you should recognize that it represents the prewar company's finest hour.

While its performance seems rather ordinary today, a two-liter car that could do 100-110mph a half-century ago was a sensation. To drive it was to experience the classic sports car in its most highly developed form. It should delight anyone who loves the marque.

In late 1936 for the 1937 model year, the Dolomite name returned on a broad range of models which ultimately replaced the Gloria and Vitesse. Frankly patterned after American design, these new Dolomites bore an ugly waterfall nose, very similar to that of the Hudson Terraplane. The roadster coupe, introduced in 1938, was so like the 1936 Mercedes-Benz 170V cabriolet that they could almost pass as twins. But the Mercedes had a traditional radiator and that seemed to make all the difference. The Dolomite's "fencer's mask" grille was so unpopular that Triumph took the extraordinary step of offering a modification: a Dolomite with a Vitesse radiator, called the Continental.

There were several Dolomite lines, but the one most worth a collector's time is the two-liter (six-cylinder) on the longest wheelbase, 116in. Aside from the grille, this is one of the most beautifully balanced cars. Its lines are not unlike the late pre-

This is Triumph's show model of the 1935 Gloria Six Flowfree sedan, a well-proportioned coupe that would be extremely desirable today, if you should find one. No Flowfree Fours were built, and the model was dropped after 1935. *Walter Belgrove collection.*

war and early postwar Jaguars (and considerably less expensive on the present-day market).

Though Dolomites have all the restoration problems of prewar Triumphs—combination aluminum and steel body panels, a vast wooden inner body structure susceptible to rot, scarce parts—they are perfectly capable of modern highway motoring. Seen from the side or rear three-quarter angle, they are impressive, the saloons having a hundred-down stance that is particularly pleasing. The best sedan is the 1939 Royal, with a slightly larger, all-steel body, sliding sunroof, flush-fitting doors, rolled and pleated leather upholstery, and wood veneer interior trim.

Though Triumph built more Glorias than Dolomites, the latter are more available in the US, and are occasionally seen in the classifieds. Unhap-

pily for the potential owner, the Dolomite Six does not enjoy "classic" status. That is reserved for the Gloria Six and the Dolomite Straight Eight only. It's an anomaly, because the six-cylinder Dolomite was every bit as expensive and exclusive as the six-cylinder Gloria. Undoubtedly the grillework influenced the CCCA.

For the advanced Triumph collector looking for something different, and willing to face a challenge, the prewar cars are enjoyable. Unlike most of their contemporaries, they are not expensive. A nice example needing only minor work can still be obtained for under five figures. There is nothing so certain to blow the minds of your fellow Triumph enthusiasts than to drive up in a Gloria, Vitesse, or Dolomite.

The 1939 Triumph Dolomite Foursome coupe in six-cylinder form is the most desirable of the Dolomite series. Except for the fencer's mask grille, the lines were magnificent from every angle. Several Dolomites are in the United States and are undergoing restoration, while quite a few more are known in Britain. Unlike the Gloria Six, the Dolomite Six is not rated as a "classic" by the Classic Car Club of America, though it would certainly seem to qualify. *Richard Langworth collection.*

For years many believed this beautiful, long-wheelbase sports saloon had never been built, but this ad from an old issue of *The Autocar* proves otherwise. It is one to look for—can it exist today? Though mounted on the Vitesse chassis, the body is believed to be the prototype for a Dolomite Straight Eight four-door model. *Richard Langworth collection.*

★★	**Razoredge Saloons**
★★	**Renown Limousine**
★★	**1800 & 2000 Roadster**
★	**Mayflower Saloon**
★★★	**Mayflower Drophead**

Early Postwar Triumphs

Razoredge Models

The Razoredge series of elegant Triumph sedans was produced in fair quantities from 1946 through 1954. Designed by Triumph's long-time body engineer, Walter Belgrove, they were truly singular cars, beautifully balanced and proportioned, and probably the only models of sub-Rolls caliber that successfully used the quintessential British body style known as razoredge or knife-edge. Like the Triumph Roadsters that accompanied them through 1949, the saloons were Sir John Black's answer to William Lyons' range of 1-1/2 liter Jaguars.

The Triumph 1800 Town & Country saloon, TD series, ran from 1946 to 1949, using the 1776cc Standard four also supplied to Jaguar. It is the least common of the saloons today, although more were made than the 2000. *Richard Langworth collection.*

Triumph's feisty managing director had supplied Lyons with engines since prewar days, and after the war Jaguar's head talked him out of the tooling for the 2-1/2 and 3-1/2 engines.

The mercurial Black decided to take out after Jaguar; to do so he used the Triumph marque, which Standard had picked up in 1943 after Triumph went bankrupt. Because of Britain's shortage of sheet steel after the war, both saloon and roadster used tubular steel chassis. Both bodies also made extensive use of aluminum in the saloons on doors and some other flat body panels. It is important to keep this in mind when you begin a restoration. Not all body shops are skilled at "prepping" aluminum, particularly at getting all the dings and ripples out; so when you're restoring a Razoredge (or a Roadster), be careful.

The first Razoredge, running the 1776cc four-cylinder engine (which Standard was still building for Jaguar's smallest-displacement model), made its debut alongside its Roadster counterpart in March 1946. It was very easy to construct the chassis for these rather-low-volume cars (the Razoredge's extra eight inches of wheelbase were had by simply extending the Roadster's main tubes), and the small-scale production was carried on at Canley. Bodies were supplied by Mulliners Ltd. of Birmingham (*not* Mulliner Park Ward, and no relation!), which furnished them painted and fully trimmed. Canley simply dropped the bodies onto the finished chassis-frames and buttoned up the lot. The initial home market price was $2,800, but the few cars imported to the States (mostly by Fergus Motors of Manhattan) went for a good $1,000 more. There were four individual series over the nine years of production, with which collectors should be familiar.

The initial TD series of 4,000 cars ran through February 1949, all with the 1776cc engine, tubular frame, transverse spring front suspension, and four-speed column-mounted gearbox. The instrument panel was the same twin-gauge arrangement of the Triumph Roadster. Though called Town & country for a while, it was more widely known as the 1800 Saloon.

In early 1949 the 1800 was superseded by the 2000 Saloon (no longer dubbed Town & Country, not yet called Renown), which was numbered in the TDA series, and 2,000 were built. Like the concurrent 2000 Roadster it retained the tubular chassis and independent front suspension, but used the new 2088cc Standard Vanguard four-cylinder engine and three-speed all-synchromesh gearbox, still column-mounted on the outboard side. Fortunately the Vanguard engine had enough torque to make this coupling possible.

Interior of the ultra rare and avidly sought-after Renown limousine of 1952, of which only 190 were built. Aside from the partition with its sliding glass window and walnut-trimmed auxiliary radio, this was the same body as on the 111in wheelbase TDC. *Richard Langworth collection.*

The third series, TDB, ran from September 1949 through December 1951; commencing November 1949 the TDB was called Renown, after one of Britain's battleships. Heavily revised from the 1800/2000, it used a modified Vanguard box-frame chassis on the traditional 108in wheelbase, with a new dashboard bearing strip-type speedometer and square minor gauges. By October 1950 the Renown had gained the "streaming torch" radiator mascot; previous cars were without mascots. The gearbox was still a three-speed, but it was now mounted on the more conventional inboard side. In January 1950, overdrive was made optional. Production was 6,500.

Fourth in the Razoredge family was the TDC-series Renown, essentially identical to the TDB but with a 3in-longer wheelbase. (The stretching applied to the *whole* passenger box; so doors, door frames, windows and interior paneling are not interchangeable between TDC Renowns and previous saloons.) This change affected all TDC saloons, but was mainly adopted for the sake of a limousine, which appeared in 1952. This rare car differed from standard only in a glass division window and walnut-trimmed radio console for the back-seat passengers. Of 190 limos, 179 remained at home while just eleven were exported. Since only one has turned up lately (in England), the odds of finding

21

From 1950 to 52, the TDB series Renown used a 108in wheelbase, the same as earlier cars, but on a box-section chassis frame. It also had a revised dashboard, though no less laden with European walnut. The TDC series from 1952 on used a 111in wheelbase. *Richard Langworth collection.*

one in the US are nil. Any limo naturally commands a very high premium.

The TDC Renown was produced through July 1954. According to factory records 2,611 were built, plus the 190 limousines. This would make the last car #TDC3111, but another source lists it as TDC 3310. Commission numbers may have been skipped, but I am inclined at present to accept the lower figure. In the US the most common saloon is the TDB, of which 814 were exported. None of the other types saw more than a few hundred exports.

For the collector the Triumph Razoredge saloon is a pleasant and interesting car, not the least because of the attention it attracts. The masses will always ask what Rolls-Royce model it is, which certainly helps your ego. The more knowledgeable know that it is no Roller, but is nonetheless an admirable four-door sedan. Its beautifully creased lines are flawless; its bright, traditional radiator grille handsome. The interior features leather-surfaced seats, thick pile carpeting, and lovely European-walnut veneer. Overdrive, which is activated by pressing the gear level downward, is an 1800, 200 or Renown, the compact Razoredge is a stunning car, and one in even fair condition is worthy of a restorer's attention.

The essential technology of a Razoredge restoration is far simpler than that of most Tri-

umphs, even the very basic, early TRs. The huge dashboard, with woodwork like a Victorian piano, comes apart and lifts out after undoing just a handful of stove bolts, and the rest of the wood veneer can easily be removed for restoration. *Caution:* This is European, not American, walnut. If any veneer has to be replaced, keep that in mind.

The technicalities of veneer restoration cannot be adequately covered here, but I *can* speak from experience. Complete refinishing with only minor reveneering, by a professional, will cost at least $1,000, and more likely twice that. If you are a good woodworker, fine—do some reading and tackle the job yourself. If not, take this into consideration or forget the Razoredge. Almost every car not previously treated needs some work in this department. Fortunately the veneer is not covered with a thick, clear coating of lacquer, but there *is* some, and it must be removed carefully to avoid disturbing the veneer.

There is more wood, ash this time, throughout the body of the car, where it forms part of the structure to which things like headliners and door panels are fixed. All this must be examined for evidence of dry rot, which is caused by a fungus call Heterobasidiomycetidae. Rotten sections must be replaced by pieces at least triple the size of the damaged section to ensure correction of this problem.

Other interior restoration is fairly straightforward on Renowns. Door panels (which are vinyl) readily come apart, but be careful and remove them gradually; obtain a parts manual and study it. Upholstery can be handled by any competent shop, but be sure to replace leather with leather, not vinyl. Series-TDB cars have headliners made of what appears to be flocked cardboard, or a substance very much like it. This material is almost impossible to restore or duplicate, and may have to be replaced with wool headliner material as used on TDC models. Before replacement, see if it responds to several coats of tan Leatherique, a water-soluble coating developed mainly for leather and vinyl by the Clausen Company (1055 King George Road, Fords, New Jersey). If not too far deteriorated, TDB headliners can possibly be saved by this excellent product, which doubles as a fine renewer material for Razoredge upholstery. The pile carpeting common to these Triumphs can be matched by many hobby suppliers.

Mechanically, Renowns are straightforward; unfortunately, few TR engine parts are exact matches. It pays to join the British Triumph Razoredge Owners Club, which can supply certain parts and tell you which TR bits *can* be exchanged. Remember, this is the 2088cc Vanguard version of Triumph's wet-liner four, not the 1991 or 2138cc TR unit; those cylinders will not mate, though they may be substituted with their liners. The Razoredge manifold is altogether different, designed for the single car—it's remarkable how this setup allows an engine that sounds very hairy in the TR to idle quietly as low as 300rpm! Many engine, chassis, and drivetrain parts are still available, mostly from UK sources, so you should develop good contacts in Britain if you acquire a Razoredge. Replacing glass is no problem (it's all flat), and the freestanding Lucas headlamp shells are common to several contemporary cars. There is little brightwork to trouble yourself over except for the bumpers and small overriders.

All sorts of prices have been quoted for Renowns, many by sellers who think they have a car of Rolls-Royce caliber. This is a gem of a Triumph, but it's no Rolls-Royce.

Remember too, that aluminum paneling aside, Razoredges do rust, particularly where the fenders join the body. The money spent on a rust-free example is well worth it in the long run.

The first of the Roadsters was the 1800 of 1946-48, which also used the 1776cc engine and tubular chassis. The bodywork was designed by two different designers who "met" at the cowl, and body paneling was all aluminum. *Richard Langworth collection.*

Designer Walter Belgrove had nothing to do with the Roadster design, but he said its back-seat passengers reminded him of "two privates perched over an Aldershot latrine." It certainly was a weird-looking rig fully laden, but here's proof that it did hold five passengers. Rear windscreen folded flat to form half of the rear deck when not is use. *Richard Langworth collection.*

1800 & 2000 Roadster

The same considerations applied to the postwar Roadster as to the Razoredge. Standard-Triumph Managing Director Sir John Black wanted a Jaguar beater, and he relied on a tubular chassis and aluminum body for it because box-section and sheet steel were in short supply. But while the saloon was a fair reply to the least expensive Jaguar saloon, the Triumph Roadster was nothing compared to the XK-120, which Bill Lyons introduced in 1948. With that, Black lowered his sights, took aim at MG and Morgan, and set his designers to work on an out-and-out sports car: First the bulbous TRX, finally the 20TS or TR1. With that, the Roadster was dropped from production.

Rich Taylor once described the Triumph Roadster, "Like Racquel Welch, buck naked, a big Navajo pendant dangling in the middle of her tawny cleavage." Perhaps this is one reason a peculiar-looking car actually designed by two different people who met in the middle has such appeal among Triumph fans. Of course, there were fewer Roadsters than Razoredge saloons, and convertibles are always more prized than closed cars, so the Roadster has a more enthusiastic following than the saloon.

The steel tube chassis had a 100in wheelbase and, like the saloon, the Roadster initially came with a 1776cc Standard engine and four-speed gearbox. To avoid sheet steel, Triumph made its body with light alloy panels formed on aircraft press tools.

The strange rear seat was the Roadster's most distinguishing feature, and it had the distinction of being the last rumble seat production car in

Britain, or for that matter the world. To get in, you climbed over the high rear fenders which, wrote Graham Robson, "must have made many a young blood very happy as he helped his girl-friend aboard."

The Roadster wasn't fast and it was certainly no Jaguar, but it did have a certain panache with its rakish, classic radiator and thirties-style "king of the road" freestanding headlamps, surmounting twin chrome-plated horns. The interior was finished similarly to the 1800 Saloon, with a huge walnut-veneered wooden dash containing two large gauges, the four-speed controlled by a right-hand-mounted column lever.

From the end of 1948, the Roadster (and saloon) received a new series designation and the Vanguard 2088cc engine, along with Ted Grinham's favored three-speed box, now controlled by a left-hand column lever. This gave it 68 instead of 63hp and, more important, a healthy boost in torque, from 92 to 108 pounds-feet, which translated into considerably more punch in the indirects and helped alleviate the wide ratios of the three-speed box.

The collector doesn't seem to prefer either model over the other, but the lower-production 2000 appears more common, perhaps because it is slightly younger. A few 2000s were imported by Fergus Motors in New York, so they're fairly—or relatively—common in the States, and there is also a free exchange back and forth across the Atlantic. The Triumph Roadster Club in England is one of the oldest one-model Triumph groups, very solidly run with a good newsletter and excel-lent parts sources, so Roadster owners have lots of company.

Aesthetically the Roadster is very much like the early TRs: You either like it or loathe it. A good one costs a hair more than a comparable Razoredge saloon, and it *is* possible to spend a five-figure amount on a really exceptional example, but be very careful in your shopping. For some reason Roadsters have been subjected to lot of customizing, and there are more nonstock examples in the US than correct ones. Many have lost their original engines, a factor that cuts the value of any given car at least in half. Quite a few have been incorrectly upholstered and painted, too, and bringing them back to original spec is expensive. Such modification is so rampant, in fact, that it pays to know what colors were actually available originally. Here they are:

1800 Roadster
    Black with beige upholstery
    Metallic gray with gray/blue upholstery
    Maroon with red upholstery
2000 Roadster
    Luminar green with green, red, or rust
        upholstery
    Champagne with gray, rust, or green upholstery
    Silver with gray, red, or green upholstery
Convertible tops
    Green cars: champagne or green
    Champagne cars: champagne
    Silver cars: gray

Andy Heighton of the Roadster Club noted that the cars were seen in many other colors including blue and white in the fifties and sixties. He met one former Triumph salesman who remembered selling a white demonstrator with blue upholstery, so the above list is not necessarily complete. Any deviation from it, however, should be viewed with suspicion.

The comments made regarding the restoration/parts situation of the saloon apply equally to the Roadster, though TRC has made a wider array of parts available. In bodywork and repaints, expert aluminum craftsmen are important, because there's even more of that metal in the Roadster than in the saloon.

An overall evaluation of the Triumph Roadster is that it's a highly collectible, not outrageously expensive open tourer, less significant historically than for its high state of quality and workmanship—a definite throwback to prewar car-building methods, with an aesthetically pleasing leather and wood interior. Styling-wise it's a quirky beast, make no mistake; yet somehow the combination of Frank Calla-

A handsome Mayflower, originally purchased by Eleanor Funk of Funk & Wagnall's, bears the Southampton, Long Island colors of ivory and black (the ivory was added by the dealer, Fergus Motors of Manhattan). The car was owned for many years by Henry Ford Museum Transportation Curator Randy Mason; it is now in North Dakota. *Richard Langworth collection.*

by's front and Arthur Ballard's back seem to hang together all right, and the dickey seat, with its unique windscreen, never fails to interest car nuts.

Mayflower

You've got to hand it to the Triumph Mayflower, and a lot of people did. When Fergus Motors offered *Mechanix Illustrated*'s famed road tester Tom McCahill a chance at one he told them, "Okay, but I want you to know I think it's a hell of a looking car and if it's half as bad as it looks I'm going to blast it wide open."

Tom duly published his verdict, calling the Mayflower an "ounce-sized English bucket" that wore its razoredge styling like "rubber boots on a ballet dancer." But he also admitted that the cute lines grew on him, that the "little book end" clocked thirty-five miles per gallon, and that it was a good value at $1,685 f.o.b. New York.

Actually it wasn't such a good buy: A new Chevy cost as much or less at the time, and this put

the curious Mayflower, designed mainly for the Americans, out in left field in the US marketplace. If nothing else, it shows how insulated some Britons were about conditions in America, and what the Yanks really wanted. Considering the Mayflower versus the TR, one is inclined to suspect that both cars, the former a failure and the latter a great success, were what they were strictly by accident.

Whatever the reasons, Sir John Black looked at the British car's early penetration into the postwar US market and decided there was a place for Standard-Triumph, too. But instead of trying to export the new, American-like Vanguard, he opted for a subcompact Triumph, choosing its name primarily to appeal to Yankee patriotism—just like Plymouth, Lincoln, Cadillac, DeSoto, Columbia and Roosevelt years before.

Whatever else you think of Rolls-type styling applied to a car this tiny, it did give the Mayflower almost unbelievable interior space. A box defines the maximum of any given space, and the

Many enthusiasts search for the ten-off drophead Mayflower, but no examples have thus far turned up. A desirable piece indeed, just bizarre enough to set collectors' juices running. *Richard Langworth collection.*

Mayflower was merely several interconnected boxes. On an 84in wheelbase (ten inches less than the Beetle) it gave four-passenger room and luggage space unrivaled by anything else up to 100 inches. One clever feature which abetted this spaciousness was the front seat design: When you tilted the backrest to enter the rear compartment, the seat itself automatically slid forward.

Very thin A and B pillars and high, wide windows gave the Mayflower excellent visibility in all directions. Because the car had a monocoque, or unitized, body-frame (one of the first), it was very tight—but collectors know that unit bodies are notorious rusters, and any car should be carefully examined for structural damage if you're thinking of buying it.

The biggest problem for Mayflower owners today is the engine which, unfortunately, was used on no other car. It was descended from, but not quite the same as, the Standard Ten: 1247cc, 38hp with detachable aluminum-alloy head and side valves operating from a four-bearing chain-driven camshaft. (*Flower power*, the name of the Mayflower club's publication, is really an oxymoron: Even the best-tuned Mayflower takes over thirty seconds to get up to 60mph, laboring through Ted Grinham's ridiculous three-speed all-synchro gearbox, borrowed from the top three gears of the Vanguard unit. Grinham staunchly believed in three rather than four speeds, but with such a small engine his theory crippled the Mayflower.)

The chassis was conventional, with independent front suspension via wishbones and coils, live rear axle with semi-elliptics, and hydraulic telescopic shocks all around. Standard equipment was lavish for a low-priced car, including a locking hood (via a clever keyhole in the mascot); locking gas cap; full set of tools including nonslip jack; fuel/oil/temp gauges; and a speedo, to which a trim odometer was added through mid-1952. Leather upholstery was optional, though Canadian cars came with a leather front seat and vinyl rear seat—if you encounter one, remember this, as peculiar as it sounds. There were trafficator directional signals, sun visors, wing vents, and underdash parcel shelf and cowl vent. In over four years of production Standard-Triumph build only 34,000 Mayflowers, and fewer than 1,000 were sold in the American market the car had set out to conquer.

In 1950 Sir John Black didn't know all this yet, and had the idea that he'd like a drophead Mayflower. The loyal Moore duly conjured one up, with an enormous soft top, blind rear quarters (it must have been hell to drive in traffic) and operating landau bars. Only ten were built, counting the prototype, and none are know at this writing. But since the Mayflower drophead remains the Holy Grail of pre-TR Triumph freaks here are the commission numbers of all ten.

TT174T4	TT215LCP
TT289LCP	TT359CP
TT438LCP	
TT441CP	TT442CP
TT443CP	TT444CP
TT353LCP	

Several dropheads have been butchered out of conventional saloons by backyard customizers, so if you hear of one and look at it, be sure to check its commission number. The Mayflower drophead is rated at three stars for its collector appeal rather than its engineering or design brilliance. It may have been an ungainly and laughable piece of iron, but there's no doubt that a complete, original car would demand a premium on today's market.

The Mayflower is the most rust-prone of any Triumph through the Spitfire, and this must be your major consideration when examining one for possible purchase. Any car exhibiting serious body rust should be avoided. If you can see the damage in place like the rocker panel or floor, you may be sure that hidden, critical places like suspension mounts are also dangerously weak.

A close second among things to worry about is the engine. Mayflowers were generally abused by US drivers, who didn't understand that these cars needed a "decoke" every 25,000 miles and weren't at all happy over 50mph. The Mayflower club *can* help with engine parts, but you should insist on a decent-running engine with proper compression in all four cylinders, and a head that is removable, not frozen through corrosion and long neglect. Chances are nine in ten that the Mayflower head which had never been off needs planing. Since the head is aluminum, that's a job best left to experts.

Minor cosmetic restoration is not difficult since most Flowers had vinyl upholstery, and the headliner and door panels were only textured cardboard. Floors came with both rubber mats and carpets, so be sure to replace the floor covering with the right material. Like the Razoredge saloons, rechroming work is minimal, even less on the Mayflower because its headlamps were built into the fenders.

Every Triumph collector who has ever owned one speaks with pleasure about the Mayflower—not because it offers high performance or luxury or driving excitement, but because it is so all-fired *cute*. Passersby stop to stare and smile at the "watch-charm Rolls," whose sheer entertainment value is rivaled by few collector cars.

Investment-wise, Mayflowers have not moved fast. The best ones still cost only $3,000-$4,000, and decent runners can be had for half that—but don't pay any less! The biggest danger here is over-restoration. It's easy to put more money into such a car than you'll ever get back.

Three of the rare TRXs were built and two survived, both in the hands of English collector John Ward. *Richard Langworth collection.*

★★★★	Long-door
★★★	Short-door
	Serial numbers
	TS1 to TS8639

TR2

This is the serious TR. This is the car real Triumph collectors restore. Enthusiasts buy the TR2 for the same reasons that people prize first edition books. The TR2 is the first of the cars that won the hearts of Americans and has now become the collector car of the TR series.

An early TR2 is the car that people would like to own if they have two Triumphs. The idea is to have a TR3B, or a TR6, for daily and weekend use. Then have one fantastic pristine TR2 for club gatherings and shows.

The TR2 is usually the second Triumph project for most of the owners. Everybody seems to start out with one of the more recent cars, because they're easier to find, and then as their Triumph enthusiasm grows they seek out the earliest possible TR.

The assignment that was handed to the Triumph staff by Managing Director Sir John Black was to produce a small sports car that could be sold at a low price. This meant taking parts off the shelf. The target price was £500, or roughly $2,000.

After World War II the British had developed sports car production to a formula. Take as many parts as possible from the mundane models and do a little tuning to raise the performance level. Then wrap all the mechanical parts in a sporty body—instant cheap sports car.

The TR's basic components were from the two-liter Standard Vanguard wet-liner four-cylinder while the chassis/frame came from the prewar Standard Flying Nine. The front suspension and the rear axle came from the Mayflower. The frame was lengthened and some structural members were added.

The basic Vanguard engine developed only 68hp but for the TR2 horsepower was pushed up to a final figure of 90hp at 4800rpm. Not a lot of horsepower by today's standards but then again coupled with the very basic (crude?) chassis it sure felt fast.

Sir John Black, chairman of Standard-Triumph, decided that the time had come to put his firm back on top of the English sports car market. With very little money, and

even less time, the 20TS, or TR1, was built. The TR1 had no trunk, but then neither did the Morgan nor the MGTD. *Plain English Archive.*

This is a restored TR2. The fender beading on these Triumphs was painted. This car had the optional front bumper over-riders installed. Don't be shocked at the price you'll pay to have the front bumper chrome plated. It will only get more expensive as the environmental restrictions on chrome plating get tougher. *Author collection.*

The body panels had to be entirely new. Walter Belgrove, who was assigned this responsibility, didn't take kindly to the traditional sports car body that was found on the MG T series. The problem was how could he come up with a new body style and spend as little money as possible. Belgrove came up with the ingenious idea of simply making the front fenders in two halves and bolting them together on the car. Not only did he keep the production costs down but he made life

Right
If you're buying an early car this is what you should check. The plate states that this car is a TR2, left-hand drive, number 1736 produced. In most states it's a serious crime to alter the VIN plate but that doesn't stop some people. *Author collection.*

a lot easier for every Triumph restorer since that day. Triumph fenders are a real joy to remove and refinish.

The cockpit area was made bigger by simply cutting the doors away. This also saved the expense of roll-up windows. The headlights were put in fixed pods that were bolted to the front of the car. Not only did all of these steps keep the initial production costs low but they also made these cars easy to restore.

Since the TR2s are considered of historic value you would be wise to try to collect the earliest possible one available. The TR2 was constantly improved as it was manufactured but none of the changes made it as nice to drive as the later TR3s. If you want a car just to drive you're probably better off selecting a TR3. The real significance of the TR2 is in its historic nature, not its performance.

The reality of this situation is that you should seek out one of the early "long door" models. Until the Fall of 1954 the TR2 was produced with doors that ran down to the bottom of the body panels. The later cars had the door cut off at the rocker panels. This change made it easier to open the door of the car when parking next to a curb, as well as strengthening the body. While this change may have made for a better car it made the early TR2s more desirable for collectors. The long door versions are the rarest of the TR series and you can expect to pay a premium price for them.

Early road testers were fairly ecstatic about the performance of the TR2—after all, they were comparing it with some rather ordinary machinery. John Bolster of Autosport acted like a child at Christmas, even praising his short-door TR2's drum brakes(which in retrospect needed improve-

An unrestored, original condition long-door TR2: the door panel extends below the chassis rails to the bottom of the body panel. This extension caused problems when getting out of the car next to a high curb. Beginning with TS4002 the doors were shortened to make opening them easier. With this stroke of practicality Triumph created the most desirable Triumph sports car of the quarter century. *Author collection.*

ment) and the top (which had to be erected in the standard British fashion). Bolster also found the optional overdrive useful but pointed out that you would only need it for flat-out runs.

A major point of disagreement was over the size of the trunk. The English thought it more than adequate while *Sports Cars Illustrated* felt it was less than acceptable, which in truth was being kind. *Sports Cars Illustrated* also felt the car was a "rocket", something no one calls the car today. They enjoyed drifting the car around corners, something which a few of us still find enjoyable. In reality maybe we don't purposely break the rear end loose often enough today. That could have something to do with the age of the owners, or the value of the car, take your choice.

From the autumn of 1954 the TR2 improvements came fast and furious. It was the classic case of engineering by Triumph, development by the customers. This means that if you fail to find a suitable long-door model look for a TR2 built in the final days. As long as you're not getting the long doors you may as well get as many improved mechanical parts as possible. For instance, from commission number TS5443 larger rear brakes were installed, which helped the brake equalization considerably.

A major difficulty TR2 owners encounter today is that it's hard to tell what parts originally came on the car. Since there's tremendous interchange between TR2 and TR3 parts, a lot of the previous owners moved parts around at random. If a TR2 part wore out it was usually replaced with a current TR3 part. I've even seen nice TR2s with wide-mouth TR3A front sheet metal. These later aprons all match up quite nicely but destroy the value of the car as a TR2. Unfortunately the original aprons are impossi-

This photo shows the long doors. This car had the standard steel wheels installed. Painted wire wheels were an option. Chrome wire wheels were never offered. *Author collection*.

An original factory photo showing a top with only one window. There are very few early photos that show long-door cars with three-window tops. *Plain English Archive.*

ble to locate these days. No one currently reproduces them and the only choice is to repair what you have, or fit something else on the car.

Other common substitutions include bumpers, overriders, cylinder heads, and early H4 SU carburetors. Even though some of these parts are currently available, TR2 owners still seem to spend an inordinate amount of time walking the rows of flea markets attempting to restore their cars to original condition. Dozens of letters get exchanged among owners seeking to discover what the original part actually looked like. It's this parts chase that makes owning a TR2 interesting.

One big change made on the TR2 was the addition of an overdrive. Beginning with TS6266, overdrive, effective on the top three gears, was made optional. Despite John Bolster's opinion overdrive is a useful option, even if it is just one more thing to go wrong. Several companies offer these units for you on an exchange basis.

Not only do you get a better cruising gear but third gear overdrive is rather nice on country roads

This is another early TR2. Notice the factory spats, or fender skirts. A company in California is reproducing these spats. They don't seem to be any more popular today than when the cars were first produced. *Plain English Archive.*

and back lanes. If gas mileage is important to you, then the overdrive will give you better mileage. If you travel on interstate highways for any length of time, the overdrive can reduce the wear on the motor as well.

There is one proviso though. The solenoid is a Lucas product. Anything from Lucas is a potential problem, but you already knew that. Before you get carried away with the mechanical parts of the overdrive, check that all the electrical parts are in good operating condition. The overdrive itself is a pretty robust mechanical device, and fails a lot less often than the actuating devices.

Owner's manuals usually advise that it's not required to change the overdrive oil frequently. This is bad advice. Knowledgeable owners change the overdrive oil when they change the engine oil. A lack of oil changes is one of the major causes of overdrive problems. Besides, the cost of an overdrive rebuild is far greater than the cost of changing the overdrive oil twice a year for the next several decades.

The other problem is that some less knowledgeable people just abuse the overdrive. Shifting into overdrive at the redline is not advised on a regular basis. Contrary to popular opinion it's not really necessary to give a TR the gas when you shift in or out of overdrive. Obviously you shouldn't use overdrive in reverse. You did know that, didn't you?

Options like overdrive were available in surprising variety on these early TRs, and they account for the wide variation you can expect in the asking prices for outwardly similar models. The lengthy option list was a part of the Triumph marketing plan. The idea was to keep the base price low, while increasing the variety available to the customer. This strategy also gave the dealers a way to add to their profit level.

Wire wheels were one of the first options offered for the TR2. Also on the list were leather upholstery (later standard), cast aluminum sump, and competition suspension (stiffer springs and shocks). Rear wheel spats (fender skirts) were

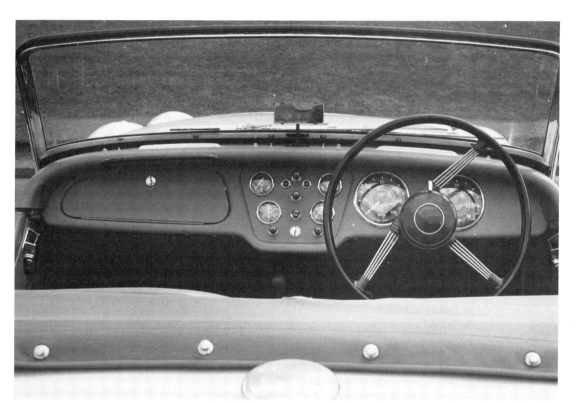

An original TR2 dash. This dash remained basically the same until the TR4. The only obvious differences were the painted grab bar, and the center section covered with the same material as the rest of the dash. Later sections were black crackle-finished. This car lacks the optional overdrive. *Plain English Archive.*

A fully restored short-door TR2. The fender beading is not correct; it should be painted. Another thing is that the top on this car is made of the wrong material. It may be a very nice top but if you plan on showing the car expect some problems. Triumph judging is becoming more demanding every year. Whenever you replace an item on your Triumph replace it with an authentic part. *Author collection.*

briefly available; these dramatically changed the looks of a TR2 or TR3. If you find a set cherish them, they may be the last set you'll see for the next decade. There is one small company in California that's reproducing them but very few people actually install them on their TR2s.

The one accessory that really changed the nature of the car was the detachable hardtop, the first of its type on a production car. The first top was introduced in 1954, and does a great deal to tighten and waterproof the passenger area. Triumph was attempting to give the TR2 more of a GT feel. The best thing it does today is let you drive the car earlier in the Spring and continue driving it later into the Fall. It really transforms the car. With a hardtop you really have two different Triumphs. Obviously, I'm a big hardtop fan.

Specific trim components for the TR2 are often scarce and require an inordinate amount of time to locate. Remember, restoring a TR2 is truly a labor of love, maybe perverted love, but love nevertheless.

The good side of restoring a TR2 is that you'll have a very small chroming bill. The only brightwork is the small inset grille. Even the fender beading is painted.

Is the TR2 a practical road car? Theoretically it should be. Like all Triumphs the thing is built like a truck. You shouldn't be too concerned about wearing it out. On the other hand you could very well damage some hard to locate component. This fear of damage is why very few TR2s get driven on a regular basis.

The standing of a long-door TR is now well established among Triumph fans. The desirability of the short-door TR2 is a little more questionable. It lacks the novelty of the long-doors and at the same time it doesn't drive as well as the later cars. The short-door TR2 is in the state of limbo. The car doesn't have the cachet of the long-door models and it isn't as nice to drive as the later TR3s. Whether to acquire a short-door TR2 depends on the purchase price and how much you love the TR2. If you find a TR2 in outstanding condition and the price is comparable to a TR3 then you should consider the car. Whether you should pay a premium price is a matter of judgment.

The time will come when the price gap between the long- and short-door TR2 widens even further. The short-door cars will be driven by their owners, and the long-door version will all be in the hands of serious Triumph collectors. With all these considerations in mind the short-door TR2 was given a rating of only one star below the early long-door cars.

There's really very little difference between the various TR2s. You particularly need to consider whether owning an early TR2 is worth the premium price, considering that the cars feel almost the same when you drive them. Today, the long-door TR2 will cost you more money to purchase. When you finally sell your prize it will bring a higher price in the market. The price differential between the early cars and the later cars will always exist. Make your choice and have some fun.

The steel trim items on the early Triumphs were painted. Triumph painted these parts to save money. The good part is that an authentic restoration will also save you money. Notice the condition of the lower windshield seal on this restored car. Purchasing a car in this condition could mean one less item that you have to have the UPS man deliver to your house. *Author collection.*

TR2
ENGINE
Type: 4-cylinder, in line, water cooled, cast iron block and cylinder head
Bore x Stroke: mm/inches: 83x92/3.27x3.62
Displacement: cc/cubic inches: 1991/121.5
Valve Operation: ohv, pushrod operation
Compression Ratio: 8.5:1
Carburetion: 2 SU H4s
BHP (mfr): 90 at 4800rpm
CHASSIS & DRIVETRAIN
Transmission: 4-speed, optional overdrive
Axle Ratio: 3.7:1
Rear Suspension: live axle, half elliptic springs, lever shocks
Front Suspension: independent front suspension, telescopic shocks
GENERAL
Wheelbase: 88"
Overall Length: 151"
Track: Front: 45"
Rear: 45.5"
Brakes: Front: 10"x2¼" drums
Rear: 9"x1¾" drums, 10"x2¼" from Fall 1954
Tire Size: 5.50x15
Wheel Size: 4x15, 4.5x15 on later cars
Weight: 1,848 lbs.
PERFORMANCE
Acceleration: 0-30: 3.4 seconds, 0-60: 11.6 seconds
Top Speed: 104mph (with overdrive)

This is an original, unrestored TR2. Note that there is no cowl vent. Over the next decade an original unrestored Triumph in this condition will be the most valuable TR2. Anyone can restore a TR2—it just takes money. An original car cannot be created, it must be discovered. A good, sound car should never be restored; it should just be maintained in original condition. There are very few of these cars available, and restoring them just creates another Triumph with reproduction parts, which are very nice cars but they aren't as rare as an original car. *Author collection.*

This motor hasn't been apart for several decades. Some of the hoses and clamps appear to have been replaced, but the rest of engine appears just the way it left England. Note the brass caps on the dash pots. Also, the pivot arms for the choke mechanism. Running a car without air filters is one sure way to wear an engine out rather quickly. On the other hand I doubt that this engine has run for several decades. *Author collection.*

★★★★	**Serial numbers TS8637 to TS13045 (drum brakes) TS13046 to TS22013 (front discs)**

TR3

This is the car everybody knows about. When you talk about Triumphs everyone just assumes you're talking about a TR3. The first TR3, which came off the Canley assembly line in October 1955, was ostensibly a new model. The differences between the TR2 and the TR3, though, really weren't all that great. Triumphs have always evolved and changes were introduced on a regular basis. Actually more

A TR3 without the GT kit lacks door handles. Note the lack of Triumph lettering, drum brakes on the front, and the 48-spoke wire wheels. *Plain English Archive.*

With the introduction of the TR3, the fender beading was made from stainless steel. Some of the changes from the early TR2 in this picture had already been incorporated into the later TR2s. There were probably more changes within the history of the TR2 than there were between the TR2 and the TR3. Note the sliding side curtains and the optional rear seat. Any number of small children have endured dangerous trips in the cramped seat. Very few normal-sized persons have allowed themselves to be subjected to a ride back there. *Plain English Archive.*

changes were made during the life of the TR2 then were between the close of TR2 production and the beginning of the TR3.

The grille was the big change. Russell Brockband, the great British cartoonist, once published a drawing of a TR2 careening madly down a winding road with a tiny tramp nestled in its vacant grille cavity. With the TR3 the tramp's nest was no more; a bold eggcrate grille was now inserted in the opening. It was an inexpensive way to alter the looks of the TR—a trick that customizers had discovered long before it occurred to Standard-Triumph. The TR3 was also the first of the TRs to use chrome hinges and shiny fender beading. With the

earlier TR2 all of these items had been covered with paint.

Outside of the brakes, the biggest change was with the engine. With a revised cylinder head, involving larger ports and larger carburetors, the engine produced 95hp. This engine was followed almost immediately by an even more potent 100hp powerplant. Triumph devotees refer to this one as the "high port head."

Yet another feature was the switch to a 4.10 rear axle ratio for the cars equipped with overdrive. This was one of the better moves Triumph made. The car felt a lot more powerful around town and by using the overdrive on the highway the revs were kept within limits. This turned out to be such a good idea that Triumph kept this rear axle ratio until the introduction of the TR7.

Another important step in the evolution of the TR3 was the introduction of Girling front brakes. Triumph was the first British manufacturer to use this braking innovation on standard production cars. Not only was this an historic breakthrough but it made the TR3 a much more practical car for normal use. Owners of TR3s can take some pride in driving a car that made braking history.

The car magazines of the era made a great deal of the fact that every Triumph was using the braking system developed for the TR2 Le Mans cars of 1955. Now, when even the lowliest of the economy cars use disc brakes the magic may not seem quite so great. Nonetheless in the fifties *Au-tosport* called them the greatest improvement ever made on a Triumph.

With the arrival of front disc brakes the rear axle was also changed. The actual gears, and the ratios themselves, were unchanged but the axle shafts were strengthened and roller bearings were used in the hubs. One more change that made the TR3 a more effective everyday car.

Triumph decided that the dealers need two models to increase sales. They found that by installing a hardtop and door handles they could sell the TR2 and the TR3 as GTs. This may have been stretching the definition a little bit, but it worked. At least Standard-Triumph thought they had two different TRs on the market. This GT kit was first used on the factory cars in the Alpine Rally. While it was offered on the TR2 it's much more common

The optional GT kit was introduced on the TR2. This option included the hardtop and the door handles. The package allowed Triumph to enter rallies and races as a GT car. The hardtop makes the car a little noisier inside but not enough to bother anyone. The advantage is that it makes the car nicer to drive in the Fall and Spring. It also means that you don't have to play with the convertible top as often. You should expect to pay more for a hardtop when you purchase a car. Make sure though, that the condition of the top justifies the higher price. Hardtops are not going to be cheap to restore. On the other hand it doesn't hurt anything to have one sitting in your basement. After you complete the restoration of the car you can start on the top. *Author collection.*

The rocker arm covers on the TR3 were chrome. Previously, on the TR2, they had been painted. Both of these engines are restored examples that have taken a lot of effort. Simply restoring an engine compartment can take as much time as you estimated for the whole car. *Author collection.*

on the TR3s. Today most of these Triumphs are not factory originals, but created from the parts shelf. There's no extra value in these cars except for the price of the hardtop, which can reach $1,000. Door handles can be ordered from parts suppliers such as the Roadster Factory or Moss Motors. Now you have your very own instant GT kit.

These hardtops are a really nice feature to have on your car. First, if you live in a northern climate it allows you to extend your driving season at least a month on each side of Summer. On those cold clear days you have no qualms about driving the car. Second, if you own a hardtop your Triumph actually becomes two different cars. Using the hardtop gives a feeling of driving a sports coupe and with the top removed you get all the fun of a Triumph roadster.

The only possible problem with a hardtop is that you get a little more noise inside the car. Instead of letting all different noises out into the atmosphere they seem to bounce around inside the car. This is really no big deal and just adds to the feeling that you have two different Triumphs. The

A TR3 from the rear. There is no lettering and the escutcheons are teardrop-shaped. This was the first time Triumph made it possible to lock something up in the trunk, but the fastener was easily undone. On the TR3A a conventional locking handle was adopted. *Author collection.*

fact these tops originally sold for $165 and now go for well over a $1,000 says a great deal about their popularity and how Triumph owners feel about the noise problem. Remember, if quiet was what we wanted then we would all be collecting Mercedes.

Another option, though one of the most dangerous and least practical, is the occasional rear seat. This seat consisted of an upholstered cushion mounted over the area behind the front seat. The very first ones were secured on special braces, but the later seats were attached to the raised and strengthened TR rear platform.

While it's possible to place small children in these seats it's foolish and illegal. Just forget that Triumph originally intended these for small children and use the space for luggage.

One option that you may never see is the fitted suitcase. In the fifties this was a common option for all sports cars but one that was seldom ordered and all of this Triumph luggage seems to have disappeared. This suitcase cost $48 back in the fifties and I can only hazard a guess as to what

one would sell for today, but be prepared to spend significant money.

How does the "small-mouth" TR3 stack up with collectors? It's a mixed feeling. The charm of the early TR2 is gone and it hasn't been replaced by the mechanical sophistication (?) of the TR3B. The TR2 has a certain allure for being the first and a early drum-braked TR3 still retains some magic for simply being an early TR3. Most TR3s still reside in that great Triumph middle ground.

When it comes to appearance the TR3 is once again in the middle. Some people like the little inset grille and others like the wider grille of the TR3A. The early TR3 basically falls into the trap of being in the middle of two very successful designs, the TR2 and the TR3A.

One of the factors here is which car you owned, or wished you had owned, when you were young. A simple fact of car collecting is that people want to buy the car they owned when they started driving. More importantly, they want to own the car they couldn't afford when they got their first driver's license. A lot of people own Triumphs out

The TR3s are often referred to as the small-mouth cars. Triumph fans feel they are less desirable than the later wide-mouth cars. One other point to look for on TR3s is that the parking lights have flat lenses. *Author collection.*

A TR3 interior. The grab bar is chromed and the center section is painted crackle-black. This car is equipped with the optional overdrive (the switch is right behind the steering wheel on the left). The radio is an accessory from the same period as the car. *Author collection.*

<table>
<tr><td colspan="2" align="center">TR3</td></tr>
</table>

TR3

ENGINE

Type: 4-cylinder, in line, water cooled, cast iron block and cylinder head
Bore x Stroke: mm/inches: 83x92/3.27x3.62
Displacement: cc/cubic inches: 1991/121.5
Valve Operation: ohv, pushrod operation
Compression Ratio: 8.5:1
Carburetion: 2 SU H6s
BHP (mfr): 95 at 4800rpm, 100 at 5000rpm on later cars

CHASSIS & DRIVETRAIN

Transmission: 4-speed, optional overdrive
Axle Ratio: 3.7:1
Rear Suspension: live axle, half elliptic springs, lever shocks
Front Suspension: independent front suspension, telescopic shocks

GENERAL

Wheelbase: 88"
Overall Length: 151"
Track: Front: 45"
       Rear: 45.5"
Brakes: Front: 11" discs
       Rear: 9"x1¾" drums, 10"x2¼" from October 1956
Tire Size: 5.50x15
Wheel Size: 4.5x15
Weight: 1,988 lbs.

PERFORMANCE

Acceleration: 0-30: 4.4 seconds, 0-60: 12.6 seconds
Top Speed: 107mph

of nostalgia. Triumphs are like 1955-57 Chevrolets—"almost everybody had one once."

On the plus side though is the fact you can locate TR3 parts a lot quicker than you can TR2 parts. This is no small consideration if you plan on using your Triumph regularly. Nonetheless, TR3 front aprons haven't been reproduced in steel at this point and the grilles are also missing from the market.

The door panels, carpeting and seats are all available as reproduction items. Fortunately the quality is now very similar to the original.

If you look at the TR3 as simply a car, and not a mechanical mistress, the TR3 is superior to any prior TR2. Disc brakes are a lot nicer for stopping than any drum-braked TR2 could ever hope to be. As long as you aren't buying the earliest possible car you may as well enjoy all the updates you can. Why not opt for the best mechanical combination that Triumph developed?

The real value of a TR3 depends on how you feel about the original TR3 styling. There's no question that the later cars are mechanically superior. Bigger motors and disc brakes are always a good idea. In a truly rational world everyone would want the latest version of the TR3, but we're not living is such an analytic world.

People buy cars because of the way they look. Styling takes precedence over performance. The TR3 is neither fish nor fowl. The serious collector will always prefer the first and the last in a series. This means that the TR2 and the TR3B will always

be the more valuable cars. The TR3 falls into a state of limbo resting between the historic early examples and the better driving cars that finished the series. On the other hand any Triumph with cutaway doors will always be more valuable than any car with roll-up windows, like the TR4.

If you are considering the purchase of a TR3, make condition a primary criterion. A really good drum brake example is preferable to a rough disc brake model. There comes a point where condition takes precedence over the model. Faced with a later TR3 in deplorable condition and an early car in outstanding condition, the car with the best condition will always win. Remember, there's more difference in driving a good and bad example of Triumph than between the TR2 and TR3B, or even a TR4 for that matter. Triumph owners love to carry on about all the differences between the various models. The real truth is that they aren't all that different. Try a Porsche if you want to experience a different type of car.

The financial difference between buying a nice car and turning a rolling basket case into a nice car is considerable. The rolling basket case will consume money like the United States government, and in the end you'll like it about as much as the withholding statement on your paycheck.

It simply can't be stressed enough. Buy the best example you can possibly afford. Enjoy the car. Drive it instead of spending three years working on it. Remember, any Triumph will present you with more than enough time to demonstrate your mechanical abilities.

This is a dash that took a lot of effort to restore. It's a fifties style rally dash. The Halda equipment was standard for the serious rallyist. Just locating this equipment today takes a lot of energy, and restoring your Triumph's dash to this condition is an even greater task. *Author collection.*

This picture shows the difference between a TR3 and a TR3A. The usual term is wide-mouth vs. small-mouth. Notice the position of the headlights on the two cars.

Whitewall tires were very common in the fifties. We're beginning to see a lot more restored cars making use of these tires. *Author collection.*

This is one of the most unusual Triumph badges around. I've only seen it on one car—a Canadian TR3. The only thing I know is that this badge was original, and came installed on the car in 1956. *Author collection.*

Chapter 5

★★★★ **Serial numbers
TS22014 to TS82346**

TR3A

This is clearly the most popular, and expensive, version of the Triumph TR series. Whole clubs have been formed to support the TR3A. Even the clubs that were formed to support all the TR2s and TR3s get most of their members from people who own wide-mouth TR3As. Some TR2 owners return home from Triumph shows wondering if they went to the right motel. This is the TR3 that everyone has in mind whenever a Triumph comes up in conversation.

The TR3A is the quintessential Triumph. There are two reasons for this. First, there are a lot more TR3As running around than any other Triumph. Second, this was really the final development of the classic TR side-curtain series. We'll get to the TR3B, which really didn't exist, in the next chapter.

Triumph had produced the ultimate TR with this series. All the engineering problems had been taken care of, at least by English standards, and the car was superior to anything in its class. Just compare the TR3A to the MGA on a summer day if you don't believe this simple fact.

The TR3A was really just a part of the evolving TR series. Only after the dealers and customers nicknamed it with the A-suffix did the factory begin using it, an official designation.

The full-width grille was the key to the whole thing. You can argue about whether or not it enhanced the TR's appearance, but it did signal that you had the latest Triumph model. At any rate there were more TR3As produced than all the TR3s and TR2s combined.

The irony of this Triumph was that it was the best of the TR3/TR2 series and the end of the line. People still enjoyed the wind-in-your-face driving style and the noisy exhaust, but not for much longer. As the TR3A lingered people began to com-

First of the wide-mouth cars, the TR3A. The front panel was totally different from the earlier cars. The grille opening was obviously larger and the headlights were set further into the panel. This is an original factory photo with whitewall tires, an item that is becoming more common on restored cars. *Plain English Archive.*

TheTR3A used letters across the rear as well as on the nose. This is the correct script for the rear of the car. The TR3A also was the first Triumph sports car to use a trunk handle. The lock cylinder was located in the center of the handle. *Author collection.*

plain about having to deal with side-curtains and something that only resembled a heater. The ride quality left people wanting a softer car. In essence people began to tire of the TR series for all the very same reasons that we collect them today.

Cars like the Sunbeam Alpine, Porsche, and Alfa Romeo, not to mention the Corvette, all had creature comforts far beyond anything the people at Standard-Triumph could imagine. Remember, you didn't buy a Triumph in 1960 to relive the past. You purchased a Triumph because it fit your image. By the early 1960s you could get the same image, better performance, and more civilized driving in a lot of other cars.

By 1960 the dealers were getting more Triumphs than they could sell. This meant that Standard-Triumph had an excess of roadster bodies for the upcoming TR3B. It also meant that TR production was slowed to a trickle of what it had been just a few years earlier.

The physical differences on the TR3A, relative to the TR3, involve more than just the grille. The headlamps were recessed further into the front fenders, appearing more streamlined—if it's possible for a TR3 to look streamlined. Door handles and a trunk latch were now made standard. Most Americans had been wondering how they could have been omitted in the first place, but then again, Triumph was never a company to dive into passing fads.

An option that was originally rare, but seems to have been installed on a lot of TR3As in the last decade is the 2.2 (actually 2138cc) engine. If you have to replace the pistons in the engine the 86mm piston/liner set is the only one worth considering. Chances are it may already be on any TR3A you're considering.

At chassis number TS56376 the front brake calipers were improved and a smaller rear brake shoe installed at the rear. This gave the later TR3As improved brake balance, but not enough that you should pay extra for this improved braking performance.

An important flaw to look for on TR3As is mismatched body panels. At TS60000 all the body

TR3A

ENGINE
Type: 4-cylinder, in line, water cooled, cast iron block and cylinder head
Bore x Stroke: mm/inches: 83x92/3.27x3.62, 86x92/3.39x3.62 optional from 1959
Displacement: cc/cubic inches: 1991/121.5, 2138/130.5 for optional engine
Valve Operation: ohv, pushrod operation
Compression Ratio: 9.1:1
Carburetion: 2 SU H6s
BHP (mfr): No official figures were stated for this motor
CHASSIS & DRIVETRAIN
Transmission: 4-speed, optional overdrive
Axle Ratio: 3.7:1
Rear Suspension: live axle, half elliptic springs, lever shocks
Front Suspension: independent front suspension, telescopic shocks
GENERAL
Wheelbase: 88"
Overall Length: 151"
Track: Front: 45"
      Rear: 45.5"
Brakes: Front: 11" discs
      Rear: 9"x1¾" drums from Fall 1959
Tire Size: 5.50x15
Wheel Size: 4.5x15
Weight: 2,138 lbs.
PERFORMANCE
Acceleration: 0-30: 4.4 seconds, 0-60: 12.6 seconds
Top Speed: 104mph

This is a nicely restored car. One item restorers should make more use of is powder paint on the bumper brackets. Powder paint is new to the restoration hobby and offers a lot of advantages over conventional paints. While it might add to the initial cost it will save you a lot of maintenance effort over the next decade. *Author collection.*

panels were changed—the first set of stamping dies had worn out. These new panels had raised pads where the hinges rested on the body panels. This was the case on both the front and rear panels. Truly fastidious collectors will avoid the cars that have the wrong replacement panels.

Triumph continued to offer a large range of minor accessories on the TR3A. These are worth looking for because they're not only useful, but they enhance the value of the car. Some of these options were offered on previous models while others are unique to the TR3A.

Two-speed wipers are distinguished at a glance by an oversize dash control knob with knurled edges, usually mounted so its lettering is ninety degrees out when the switch is off. The actual two-speed motor is no longer available so this may be one of those little items that'll make your TR3A special, if the motor actually works.

The optional adjustable steering wheel was continued from the TR3. Adjustments were made by twisting a collar around the steering column. The actual wheel itself is even different. The space between the individual springs of the "sprung" steering wheel are slightly wider and these arms form a definite Y-shape. Standard steering wheels have the spokes closer together and the two upper arms of the Y slope down, not up.

Even in the lowest position this adjustable steering wheel sets closer to the driver's chest than the nonadjustable version. Just to complicate matters a little more the upper arms of the adjustable steering wheel block some of the gauges. What we have then is a not very useful accessory, but one that still has a certain novelty appeal. After all, who ever said that old car nuts were really rational people.

The desirable options are the racing options, especially the special windscreen and the Alfin aluminum rear brake drums. Also, there were some alloy oil pans and skid plates offered. All these items are very rare today; buy them anytime you get a chance.

The two rarest options are the special leather suitcase and the rear wheel fender skirts, or spats, as the English prefer. I've actually seen the fender skirts, but doubt if any suitcases still exist.

The optional leather interior was no longer offered since the seat surfaces came with leather already installed. The seat itself was actually revised

The headlights are different on this English model. Other than this difference, the front is exactly the same. Tri- umph was spelled out across the front of the car. *Plain English Archive.*

and offered a more curved back. This happened after TS 22013 and was installed on all cars with TCF and TSF commission numbers.

It's important to remember that you can de- stroy the value of a TR by replacing a worn-out in- terior with cheap vinyl, or PCV. A cheap interior, with ill-fitting seat covers, will convince people that a heathen owned this TR, the conclusion being that the rest of the car is in as bad a condition as the seat. Always replace the upholstery with the same type of material that was originally installed at Standard-Triumph. Spend the money it costs to do the job properly.

Carpeting is another area where you need to be careful. The original carpeting is gone from this world. Any TR you're considering will have had the carpeting replaced several times. On the TR3A Triumph used a cheap loop-weave carpeting. The carpeting on all previous TRs was a quality wool carpet with a short tight pile. The change to the cheaper carpeting took place around TS35350.

Carpeting is one area where the reproduction materials are questionable. Some suppliers are sell- ing carpeting very close to the original while others are selling whatever comes close. Before you pur- chase any carpet set make sure that you ask for a

This is the type of car that's bound to give concours judges fits: it's beautifully restored, but it has the wrong top. This type of top was originally used on the early TR2. The problem with the TR2 convertible top is that visibility was poor. (In spite of the visibility problems, though, there will be more and more of these tops in-stalled on TR2s as Triumph owners return the cars to original condition.) Another item that's becoming more popular each year is the original style whitewall tires. The knock-off hubs on this car are also obviously from too recent an era, as they lack the stock knock-off ears. *Author collection.*

sample. If the company won't send this sample check with another Triumph supplier.

While on the subject of carpeting please note that carpeting was not installed on the floor in front of the seats. Only the early TR2s had carpeting in this area. Triumph used rubber mats on all the other Triumphs, rubber mats which are not available today. If you have an original set of rubber mats—save them. No matter what sort of condition they might be in these are valuable items.

Another item where you need to use caution is in the replacement of tops and side curtains. These items are available in material that is very close to the original vinyl. On the other hand there are a lot of cheap reproductions on the market. The best advice here is to ask the people who win all the trophies at the Triumph shows where they buy their tops. Never purchase side curtains or tops without getting a lot of advice from people who have already gone through the process.

With a total production of 61,567, the TR3A will never be among the rare collectible cars. At first glance the TR3A would appear less desirable than the TR3. This is a case where the numbers don't tell the whole story.

The big reason is that the TR3A is a better car than the TR3. The overall engineering is better and the car is actually easier to drive. The vast majority of Triumph owners seem to like the TR3A better than the TR3. Just keep in mind that collecting Triumphs is not a wholly rational enterprise. That means you should forget all the little nuances and simply buy the car you like best.

Another TR3A, this time with the correct top and knock-off hub nuts. The nose badge remained exactly the same from the TR3 to the TR3A. *Author collection.*

This is a rare item. This alloy wheel is an original TR3 option. This wheel has obviously been restored. If you can locate a set of these wheels plan on paying big dollars. The Panasport wheels look similar to these wheels but there are enough differences so that reproductions will never take the place of the real thing. *Author collection.*

The hardtop was one of the rarer accessories. It will also be one of the last items to be reproduced. The value of the TR-series hardtops can be expected to rise faster than the value of the cars themselves. *Author collection.*

Another TR3A with the whitewall tires. The top is also the correct style for the model, as are the knock-off hubs. This Triumph is the most expensive on the market; it will also be the most expensive ten years from now. Price is determined by options and condition. *Author collection.*

Hard top...soft life!

The living is easy in a Triumph TR-3 Grand Touring Model. (Witness this lucky Las Vegas driver.)

The steel hard top is readily detachable. But so many people like its smart looks and year 'round comfort they just don't take it off. Hard top or not, the TR-3's nimble handling and orthopedically designed seats make you forget the miles and enjoy the fun of driving.

Everything about the Triumph TR-3 Grand Touring Model is "grand" but the price. It costs $500 less than any comparable sports car...gives up to 35 miles per gallon.

The TR-3 has won 1st in class in countless rallies on both sides of the Atlantic. So it's not surprising it's America's number one selling sports car.

The soft life begins at your Triumph dealer. See him today for a test drive!

TRIUMPH TR-3
GRAND TOURING $2835*

6 reasons why the TR-3 is U.S.A.'s #1 sports car buy:

1. *DISC BRAKES:* Standard equipment on front wheels for maximum braking efficiency; will not fade, grab or lock.

2. *1991 cc. ENGINE:* 100 horsepower; top speed: 110 miles per hour; acceleration: 0-50 in 8 seconds.

3. *GEARBOX:* 4-speed; short throw for easy shifting; heavy duty synchromesh in 2nd, 3rd and top offers rugged, smooth operation.

4. *FRAME:* Rigid "X" type for stability; rust-proofed steel.

5. *HAND BRAKE:* Racing type—centrally mounted; has quick release "throw-off" action.

6. *RACING CLUTCH:* Heavy duty woven lining for longer life.

OPTIONAL EXTRAS: Overdrive, soft top kit, rear seat, wire wheels, white walls and others (ask your dealer).

SERVICE: Dealers in every state — over 700 of them in all.

*Convertible model, $2675. (At U.S. Ports of Entry, plus state and/or city taxes—slightly higher West Coast.) Standard-Triumph Motor Company, Inc., Dept. F-20, 1745 Broadway, New York 19

Author collection.

54

This is one of the nicest Triumphs you can purchase. This is an original condition car. You can't make a TR3 like this. It would be a shame to restore a car like this. They have to acquire the patina. Triumph clubs have to give some serious thought to having a "Survivor Class" at their Summer gatherings. This class would be for original condition cars only. *Author collection*.

Thar's GO
in them thar hills!

The Triumph TR-3 scampers up *and down* the meanest mountain road without getting winded.

Why?

Because its engine, steering, suspension and disc brakes are designed for car-killing European road competition. (The TR-3 has taken first in class in practically every European Rally during the past five years.)

Those of you interested in less strenuous virtues will like the fuel economy (up to 35 mpg), the ortho-pedically designed seats and the *fun*. All are stand-ard equipment.

Drive a TR-3. It handles so easily, your wife will want to keep it for herself. And, best of all, it costs $500 less than any comparable sports car.

Spring is here. Why wait?

Standard-Triumph Motor Company, Inc., Dept. F-59,1745 Broadway, New York 19

Author collection.

Chapter 6

TR3B

★★★★★ TSF
★★★★★ TCF
Serial numbers
TSF1 to TSF530
 (all-synchro gearbox)
TCF1 to TCF2804
 (TR4 engine)

This is the TR3 that really didn't exist. At least it was the TR that Triumph never planned to make. When the TR4 was introduced to the North American dealers they expressed a great deal of doubt about whether they could sell the car. Triumph

buyers didn't want roll-up windows and modern body styles. At least they weren't prepared to pay for them.

In an effort to appease these dealers Standard-Triumph decided to produce one last round of

The TR3B is so similar to the TR3A that in the factory picture files they are listed TR3A/B. They were only sold in North America, as a hedge against the introduction of

the TR4. They are also the best driving of the TR3 series. Especially nice is the TR4 engine of the TCF series. *Plain English Archive.*

```
TR3B—TSF SERIES
ENGINE
Type: 4-cylinder, in line, water cooled, cast iron block and
    cylinder head
Bore x Stroke: mm/inches: 86x92/3.268x3.622
Displacement: cc/cubic inches: 1991/121.5
Valve Operation: ohv, pushrod operation
Compression Ratio: 9.1:1
Carburetion: 2 SU H6s
BHP (mfr): 95 at 4800rpm
CHASSIS & DRIVETRAIN
Transmission: 4-speed, optional overdrive
Axle Ratio: 3.7:1
Rear Suspension: live axle, half elliptic springs, lever
    shocks
Front Suspension: independent front suspension, tele-
    scopic shocks
GENERAL
Wheelbase: 88"
Overall Length: 151"
Track: Front: 45"
        Rear: 45.5"
Brakes: Front: 11" discs
        Rear: 9"x1¾" drums
Tire Size: 5.50x15
Wheel Size: 4.5x15
Weight: 2,138 lbs.
PERFORMANCE
Acceleration: 0-30: 4.4 seconds, 0-60: 12.6 seconds
Top Speed: 104mph
```

```
TR3B—TCF SERIES
ENGINE
Type: 4-cylinder, in line, water cooled, cast iron block and
    cylinder head
Bore x Stroke: mm/inches: 86x92/3.386x3.622
Displacement: cc/cubic inches: 2138/130.5
Valve Operation: ohv, pushrod operation
Compression Ratio: 9.0:1
Carburetion: 2 SU H6s
BHP (mfr): 100 at 4600rpm
CHASSIS & DRIVETRAIN
Transmission: 4-speed, optional overdrive
Axle Ratio: 3.7:1
Rear Suspension: live axle, half elliptic springs, lever
    shocks
Front Suspension: independent front suspension,
    telescopic shocks
GENERAL
Wheelbase: 88"
Overall Length: 151"
Track: Front: 45"
        Rear: 45.5"
Brakes: Front: 11" discs
        Rear: 9"x1¾" drums
Tire Size: 5.50x15
Wheel Size: 4.5x15
Weight: 2,138 lbs.
PERFORMANCE
Acceleration: 0-30: 3.9 seconds, 0-60: 12.1 seconds
Top Speed: 107mph
```

TR3s. The fact they had a supply of TR3 bodies laying around the Canley factory also helped make this decision an easy one. (Too bad Triumph didn't have a few extra TR6 bodies when they introduced the TR7.)

This TR3 body supply ran out after the 3,300th TR3B was completed, the result being the most desirable TR3. Remember, the last of a series is always the most coveted.

The TR3Bs were produced by the Forward Radiator Company from the same tooling used by Mulliners Ltd., who had produced the TR2/3. In fact, Mulliners shipped the tooling to Forward Radiator. The first 530 cars were virtually indistinguishable from the TR3A, the only difference being the commission number. They used the 1991cc engine but almost of them were mated to the all-synchromesh TR4 gearbox. These are nice cars but then Triumph went on and produced an even more desirable TR3.

The TCF-series TR3B is probably the high water mark of the TR3 series. This is the most collectible and will always be the most valuable. If

you're serious about collecting Triumphs with cut-down doors only this car and the long-door TR2 will suffice.

The TCF series was fitted with the 2138cc TR4 engine and the TR4 all-synchro gearbox. This was the best drivetrain fitted to the TR3.

The TCF was really created out of leftover parts and the cars are always a little different. There were mismatched colors and the fit and finish were surely not up to the level of a new TR4. This can all be corrected during a restoration, if somebody hasn't done it already. Whether you need to mismatch the trim in the interior is a subject for the next Triumph workshop.

The British never really liked these cars, but that may have been because they were never able to purchase them. The TR3B is truly an American car.

A TR3B is still the best TR3 to restore, especially the TCF series. You should keep in mind that these cars are great drivers and hopefully they won't be relegated to the role of trailered show cars. They're just the best of the TR3 series, not works of art that have to be sequestered.

Since the TCF series had the TR4 motor, the oil filler hole should be toward the rear of the car. The valve cover is correctly chromed and the manifold is correct. *Author collection.*

Here is a TR3B that never had its Triumph lettering installed across the front. A number of the late cars in this series lacked the lettering. Apparently the factory ran out of letters and didn't bother to order new ones. Just to confuse the situation, some TR3Bs had TR4-style lettering across the nose. The lettering on the nose of TR3Bs will always be one of those points of controversy and endless discussion. *Author collection.*

TR4

This is a car that doesn't get the respect it deserves. The TR4 is a big improvement over the TR3 but the legions of TR3 fans have consistently refused to acknowledge that simple fact.

The TR4 gets very little admiration because of the fact it's not a TR3. The TR4 is stuck between two of the most desirable Triumphs on the market, the TR3B and the TR6. We're talking about a car that offers neither the classic TR3 looks nor the power of the TR6. The car gets glossed over as being neither. The only way to deal with a TR4 is to consider it on its own terms.

The design was handled by Triumph's new styling consultant, Giovanni Michelotti. The purists were shattered: not only was there no place to rest your elbows but the car arrived with roll-up windows! *Plain English Archive*.

This is a very early TR4 dash. The owner has had this car since it was new. The large vents on the ends of the dash work very well. In fact they work a lot better than the "eye-balls" on the TR6. The steering wheel cover on this car is an obvious addition. Steering wheels can be very difficult to restore, and expensive to replace, so always check to see what's under the cover. *Author collection.*

The problem for the collector is that while you can buy a TR4 for a reasonable price it's going to cost you as much as a TR3 or TR6 to restore. Without even trying you've invested more money and effort in the car than it'll ever be worth.

The TR4's major problem was that it was a step into the modern era. The lack of side curtains and a modern body do little to bring back memories of the fifties. The TR4 suffers from being just a little too modern.

On the other hand collectors will be quick to tell you that it lacks the sophistication of the TR6. The reality of it was that the TR4 was produced with more quality than the TR6. Triumph never again reached the build quality of the TR4.

All the prejudice against the TR4 means that you can get a nice roadster for a reasonable price.

Even better you might consider the TR4 as a daily driver. There's no reason why this car couldn't be used every day.

The TR4 only seemed like a new car when it was introduced. Everything but the body was taken straight from the TR3 parts shelf. Mechanically the TR4 is not much more sophisticated than the TR2. It's just that windows which roll up and down puts a lot of the vintage Triumph people off.

The TR4 engine was the same 2.2 option that was installed in the TR3A. Conversely, you could also order a special 1991cc engine to compete in the under 2-liter racing classes. Needless to say very few were ever built and they have no special importance today.

The transmission was changed so that first gear was synchronized. This alone makes the TR4

TR4

ENGINE

Type: 4-cylinder, in line, water cooled, cast iron block and cylinder head

Bore x Stroke: mm/inches: 86x92/3.386x3.622

Displacement: cc/cubic inches: 2138/130.5, 1991cc engine available as a no-cost option

Valve Operation: ohv, pushrod operation

Compression Ratio: 9.0:1

Carburetion: 2 SU H6s, 2 Strombergs on later cars

BHP (mfr): 100 at 4600rpm

CHASSIS & DRIVETRAIN

Transmission: 4-speed, optional overdrive

Axle Ratio: 3.7:1

Rear Suspension: live axle, half elliptic springs, lever shocks

Front Suspension: independent front suspension, telescopic shocks

GENERAL

Wheelbase: 88"

Overall Length: 153.6"

Track: Front: 49"

Rear: 48"

Brakes: Front: 11" discs

Rear: 9"x1¾" drums

Tire Size: 5.90x15

Wheel Size: 4.5x15

Weight: 2,200 lbs.

PERFORMANCE

Acceleration: 0-30: 3.5 seconds, 0-60: 11.5 seconds

Top Speed: 110mph

worth considering. The truth of the matter is that any number of TR3s have had this transmission installed. Overdrive was offered as an option with the switch now controlled from a handy lever on the dashboard. As in the past, when you ordered the overdrive you received the 4.11:1 rear axle ratio. Overdrive remains a desirable option and is still a useful thing to have, provided you maintain it properly.

Despite the all-new body, the early TR4's appointments and behavior resembled the TR3. The instruments are spread across the dash, even down to the black crackle-finish panel for the four smaller gauges in the center. The carpet in the TR4 came in one color only—dark charcoal gray. It was a loop-pile type.

The bucket seats on the early TR4s were really straight from the TR3A. They were changed to a flatter design for the later cars. All the proper upholstery is available from one of the various parts suppliers. When the seats were changed the dash was also revised. The black finish was covered in a walnut veneer. This veneer usually cracked and separated with time.

The TR4 was a very well planned and executed sports car. For years people had complained about the lack of ventilation in the TR3. For the TR4, Triumph incorporated two large fresh-air vents in the outer edges of the dash. They installed

The TR4 used two small lights in the grille and had no brightwork on the sides of the car. *Plain English Archive.*

two big roller wheels to control these vents and linked them directly to the cowl vent (which also has to be open when the heater is turned on). These interior vents allow a lot of fresh air into the interior. Unfortunately they do it in the winter as well, even when closed. For the first time Triumph tried to give the owner of the TR4 a decent heating system. They even installed a temperature control knob, as well as the blower control knob. There was also a directional knob that allowed you to duct air towards the windshield. A real defroster in a Triumph! Would miracles never cease? Of course, "real" is a relative word.

The other item that everyone loved was the real trunk, which was large enough for several suitcases. The rack and pinion steering was also a welcome change. This was a big improvement over the old worm-and-roller steering. There's a direct positive feel to the TR4 that no previous TR can match.

The TR4 even seemed to ride better. Standard-Triumph took the time to install some bracing between the cowl and the transmission area. No longer did the whole cowl shake like an asthmatic cow as you drove over rough roads.

The TR4 was a much improved car, and saved the company—at least for a short time. However, this was not a perfect car by any standard. People complained about the antique top, which was one of those classic British top kits. The good part is that today it's probably a good deal. I like the idea that you can carefully remove the top and store it away for the summer. Modern folding tops actually present more problems for the classic car owner.

The other complaint was about the cheap stamped grille. People thought that something more substantial would have been appropriate. Once again the very cheapness should make them easy to reproduce. I say should because right now there seems to be a problem getting anyone to reproduce them.

When the TR4 was seriously raced it was unbeatable in its class. Compared to the TR3 it was a major leap into the sixties. In fact a TR4 with a racing history will be the most valuable example you might locate.

One important point to consider is the fuel system on the TR4. The Zenith Stromberg carbs that were fitted to some of the TR4s are a problem. Most shops would rather deal with the SU H6 carburetors. They just seem simpler. In reality it's just a matter of having patience and spending a fair amount of time learning about them.

The best TR4 arrangement is to buy a set of Webers. These are wonderful. The only thing to be careful about is that you buy them from someone

The hood blister on the early TR4s was shorter than on the later cars. Also, if you go around to the back of the hood you'll find that the hood latch is different. *Author collection.*

The first TR4 production line in operation during the Fall of 1961. The new car was built at the then-new Standard-Triumph Liverpool plant in Speke. *Plain English Archive.*

who is willing to help you get them running properly. The nice thing is that once you get a set of Webers set up properly you should never have to touch them again. I have a set that I haven't done a thing to for five years. It did take two months of experimentation to get the car running properly though.

One variation that merits more serious consideration is the Surrey Top TR4. This is a unique feature that was never found on any other Triumphs. The Surrey Top was designed by Giovanni Michelotti (who also created the basic TR4 design) as a predecessor to the Targa top. The rear window, with a light alloy frame, was attached to the top of the body. Then, between this rear window frame and the front windshield a roof panel was installed. The removable metal panel was installed at the factory, but the only problem was that it couldn't fit in the trunk. A non-portable portable top. Great.

The soft top is the one that everyone uses. This folds up and fits in the trunk. The good news is that parts for this Surrey Top are being repro-

This is the Surrey Top. This owner has been looking for the metal section that goes over the middle for over a decade. The snaps are not original. When the original top wore out some owner simply replaced it with a vinyl and snaps. Something unique like the Surrey Top enhances the value of the TR4, but at the same time it adds a lot problems when you try to do a proper restoration. *Author collection.*

duced. There are still some items that aren't available but the situation is getting much better.

Very few of these cars came to the United States. If you're going to restore a TR4 this may be the only car that can justify the cost of restoration. It's been estimated that this top will increase the value of a TR4 by 25 percent. The other big benefit is that they cut down the wind at highway speed.

The basic problem with the TR4 is that it's really too conventional. Think about what the headlights did for the Bugeye Sprite. Would the TR3s be

in such demand without the cut-down doors?

You might even want to think of the TR4 as a TR3 with a modern conventional body. It has all the good features of the TR3, plus some extra benefits, without the unique look. There's really only one reason to not own a TR4—it will never be as popular as the earlier cars. This means that you'll spend just as much money restoring the car but the end value will be lower than a nice TR2 or TR3.

This is the sort of TR4 to avoid. If you even think about buying a car in this condition get your parts catalog out and start adding up the cost of parts. This type of car will ultimately be the most expensive TR4 that you can purchase. *Author collection.*

When you see this sort of rust on a Triumph it's like looking at an iceberg—you're only looking at the upper 10
percent of the problem. This is not simply a cosmetic
problem. It's going to take a lot of effort to bring this car
back to life. *Author collection.*

What does it take to beat the Triumph TR-3?

The Triumph TR-3 is the most popular sports car in America. It practically started the sports car boom. A hard car to beat. But wait till you see Triumph's new one, the TR-4. It has all the power of its famous companion. But it's even more exciting to drive and easier to handle. The torque (engineer-talk for the thrust developed at any given speed) is high at all speeds. So, unlike many other sports cars, the TR-4 does equally well at a modest 50 or a thundering 100. The track is wider, so the TR-4 corners flat as a pancake. The TR-4 is easier to control, too. The new steering system is as effortless as power steering, but far more responsive. And shifting in motion, even to 1st, presents no problems. The TR-4 has synchromesh on all forward gears. P.S. The windows roll up. The top locks in place to rain-proof the interior. And the price is a mere $2849.* ■ The only real way to find out about the TR-4 is to get behind the wheel and hit the road. There are Triumph dealers in every state of the union — including Hawaii and Alaska. One lives near you. Drop in and **TRIUMPH** ask him for a test drive. Discover for yourself how much more fun driving can be.

*P.O.E., plus state and/or local taxes. Slightly higher in West.
U.S.A.: Standard-Triumph Motor Co., Inc., Dept. E-22, 1745 Broadway, New York 19, N.Y.
CANADA: Standard-Triumph (Canada) Ltd., 1463 Eglinton Avenue West, Toronto 10, Ont.

Author collection.

Chapter 8

TR4A

★★★	IRS
★★★★	Live axle cars
	Serial numbers
	CTC50001 to
	CTC78684 (IRS)
	CT prefix only for
	live-axle cars

If the TR4 gets too little respect the TR4A gets even less. Most people simply regard this as a TR4, if they even realize it exists at all. The TR4A is really an important step in the evolution of the TR series.

Whether you want to own one is a completely different question.

The TR4A, introduced in 1965, featured the TR's first independent rear suspension (IRS). This

Once again the changes were very minor. The raised turn signal/running light was new, as well as the metal spear along the side of the car. The grille was an improvement. *Plain English Archive.*

This is another picture of the grille. Notice the lack of hood lettering on this car. It was delivered this way. I've never quite figured out why some cars got lettering and others didn't. *Author collection.*

IRS was patterned after, but not exactly the same as, the Triumph 2000 saloon. The TR4A retained the lever shocks even though the Triumph 2000 used the more effective tubular shocks. Time moved slowly at Triumph.

The IRS chassis received a massive steel bridge to support the differential, as well as a place to put the coil springs. With this new rear the TR4A Triumph was the only British manufacturer with a complete line of independent rear suspended cars. Every Triumph came with four wheel independent suspension, except for the American market.

When the TR4A was introduced the American Triumph dealers didn't want the car. These American dealers felt that they couldn't justify the price increase of the TR4A to their customers. Thus, the IRS became a option in the United States. This was probably one of the few times that a rear suspension option was available, anyplace.

What didn't become an option though was the new frame. It would've been too much even for Triumph to offer optional frames. An optional TR4 frame was simply out of the question so Triumph found a way to attach a solid axle to the new TR4A frame.

Car and Driver, along with others, couldn't figure out why the IRS wasn't made standard. They called it "one of the wildest options ever offered by any manufacturer." All of the magazines went out of their way to praise the new Triumph rear suspension. Then again Triumph bought a lot of ad space in all these magazines.

The reality is that this IRS technology really wasn't necessary. American roads are fairly straight and under most conditions you'll be hard pressed to identify which rear end you actually have under the car.

If you have to have any work done on the rear end the costs will be considerably more for the IRS

69

This is a quality restoration. There are no rust pits in the chrome, and the gaskets have been replaced. *Author collection.*

TR4A

ENGINE
Type: 4-cylinder, in line, water cooled, cast iron block and cylinder head
Bore x Stroke: mm/inches: 86x92/3.622x3.386
Displacement: cc/cubic inches: 2138/130.5
Valve Operation: ohv, pushrod operation
Compression Ratio: 9.0:1
Carburetion: 2 Stromberg 175 CDs
BHP (mfr): 105 at 4700rpm
CHASSIS & DRIVETRAIN
Transmission: 4-speed, optional overdrive
Axle Ratio: 3.7:1
Rear Suspension: independent rear suspension, coil springs, semitrailing arms, lever arm shocks
Optional on US cars: live axle, half elliptic springs, lever shock
Front Suspension: independent front suspension, telescopic shocks
GENERAL
Wheelbase: 88"
Overall Length: 153.6"
Track: Front: 49"
      Rear: 48.5"
Brakes: Front: 11" discs
      Rear: 9"x1¾" drums
Tire Size: 6.95x15
Wheel Size: 4.5x15, wire wheels optional
Weight: 2,245 lbs.
PERFORMANCE
Acceleration: 0-30: 2.9 seconds, 0-60: 9.8 seconds
Top Speed: 104mph

than for the straight axle TR4A. The irony here is that the American dealers may have been right when they objected to the IRS.

Currently there's very little difference in the value between a TR4 with the IRS and one without it. Considering the cost of any possible problems in the rear you probably should look for a TR4A with an old-fashioned straight axle.

The engineering staff had also considered boosting the power of the TR4A by using a 2.5 liter dry-liner engine but tests proved this combination produced very little increase in horsepower. We ended up with the 2.2 liter engine but with about 4 additional horsepower. This was the final development of the TR four-cylinder engine, certainly the best of all the TR engines. Any number of them have found their way into TR3s, which makes a nice, if not historically correct, combination.

Turning away from the mechanical aspect, the TR4A perfected the basic TR4 package. The cheap, stamped-aluminum grille, which had been around since the TR3, was replaced by a more substantial tube grille. The running lights were moved into little chrome nacelles on the front fenders, along with the amber turn-signals for the directional lights. The US-market cars had the European signals painted black. If you want the Euro look simply scrape the black paint away from the inside of the lens and install a bulb in the socket.

The only other item altered on the exterior were the badges. A red and gray plastic globe in a chrome surround replaced the traditional Triumph open-book badge on the hood. The only problem was that this plastic usually faded out so quickly that you ended up buying a new one every couple of years. On the other hand you could just keep your Triumph out of the sun.

Inside, the polished walnut dash was retained but the overdrive switch was moved from the right to the left under the steering wheel. Its place was taken by a headlight/side lamp/flasher lever. The seats, which had been very flat on the later TR4s, were given more of a bucket shape again. Vinyl trim pads were added to the window edges. The TR4A center console/dashboard brace was now padded. No longer did you have to bang your knee on the sharp metal frame.

The TR4A top became more of a problem. The top was permanently fixed to the metal frame and was easier to operate in a hurry. Unfortunately, this top takes up at least half the space behind the seats when lowered. The original complicated top on the TR4 at least had the advantage of being neater to stow away, and allowed room for more luggage.

The luggage rack was a very popular option. This car also had the optional IRS suspension. At least it appears that way. Don't assume that the IRS is present under this car—look to make sure. *Author collection.*

The TR4A was a far more sophisticated car than the old TR4. The big difference was underneath where there was an all-new frame and, on some models, independent rear suspension. This suspension, an option in the United States, is also one more thing to give you trouble on an older Triumph. *Plain English Archive.*

One of the nicest TR4A restorations in the country. This view also clearly shows the new parking light arrangement and the side spear. This type of restoration was clearly a labor of love, as its cost was probably more than the car is actually worth. The price of the chrome wire wheels alone put this one in a special category. If you embark on a project like this, be realistic. You're doing it as a hobby, not to make money. *Author collection.*

The TR4A used these unreliable Stromberg 175CD carburetors which were introduced during the TR4 model run. The later TR4A reverted back to SU HS6s, the same as the earlier TR4. There's no difference in performance, but the SUs are far preferable. The horsepower was up to 140hp at 4700rpm. *Author collection.*

Driving a big four-cylinder Triumph is always fun. Angled back in the bucket seat, which is much less upright than the TR2/TR3, you gaze across what seems like an acre of hood. The big bump on the hood gives you the feeling of power even though it was only needed to clear the carbs on the earliest cars.

You can start the engine with a key on the TR4A instead of starter button. Shifting is fun because there's a precision that no modern sports car seems to match. You can get to 60mph in just under eleven seconds, not real exciting, but it sounds so neat, and generally the car is doing all sorts of bouncing and jumping around while you pretend to go fast.

The big bore Triumph four-cylinder engine has enough torque to give you the feeling of speed. This is no high-winding Japanese engine. This is a big solid car with great big pistons that create wonderful noises. It's a package that's really quite modern, and one that seems to be more fun every time you drive a well prepared example.

At the same time the TR4A is an enigma. It's a very good car that's attracted almost no attention from the collectors. The TR3 fanaticism is so strong that the TR4A isn't really considered. People who like the modern TR4A body style usually opt for the TR6, or the TR250, with more power. The TR4 is the car that no one gets serious about.

The problem is that you're going to spend roughly the same amount of money to restore a TR3, a TR4A, or a TR6. The TR4, or 4A, will always be worth less money when it comes time to sell the car.

From a financial standpoint you should think twice before you restore a TR4A. On the other side it's still a very nice car. Parts are readily available. In fact there are very few parts unique to the TR4A. A lot of the running gear was carried over to the TR250. The parts that weren't used on the 250 were probably left over from the TR3.

There's an outside chance that these carbs can be rebuilt. This is what happens when a car sits outside for about a decade. *Author collection.*

Chapter 9

★★★   **Serial numbers
CP1 to CP3096**

TR5 PI

The TR5 may very well be the best TR4 on the market. What we have here is a TR4 with a six-cylinder engine. It was one way to test out your new motor and pretend that you've just developed a new car. Whatever, it's definitely one of the rarest Triumphs. The TR5 PI (Petrol Injection) was never officially imported into the United States. The few that made it to North America went to Canada. Then there were the few hardy people who imported them into the United States as individuals.

The English have never really appreciated this car. The trouble was that they didn't get stuck with the TR250. Maybe the real reason all of us in the United States like the car is that we can't have one.

The quest for more Triumph power was certain to lead to a six-cylinder engine. The only problem was that Triumph didn't have a six-cylinder engine with enough horsepower to justify the change. The 2-liter/GT6 engine produced even less horsepower than the TR4A engine.

Chief engineer Harry Webster took the unorthodox route of adding two cylinders to the old four-cylinder engine. When this still didn't produce enough horsepower he went to a fuel-injection system. This Lucas system was already under consideration as a way to meet the emission standards for the United States.

The PI engine cranked out 150hp at 5500rpm and gave the TR5 tremendous performance. It was

Wire wheels are the only way to suspend the TR5/250: the steel wheels with their silly hubcaps destroy its looks. If you have to make a change, find a TR4A with correct parts in a junkyard and swap. Buying all-new parts can be very expensive. *Plain English Archive.*

the fastest TR ever. This performance didn't come cheap. *Car* magazine placed the cost of the fuel injection system at roughly eight times what a set of SUs might have cost. Triumph explained that this expense was necessary to satisfy the performance fans in the European market who demanded all the extra power. In fact there was no such Triumph market in Europe, and the TR5 did nothing to create a market. The PI car was a glorious failure with fewer than 3,000 cars produced.

The final irony of the TR5 PI was that it couldn't pass the American emissions requirements. This meant that America never saw the car. We got the Zenith Strombergs which gave the TR250 the same horsepower as the TR4A.

The TR5 never even caught on in the English market. After all, the TR4 shape had been around for more than seven years and the car still only had a top speed of 117mph. If you got the overdrive you might be able to break 120mph. The overdrive being worth 5 more miles per hour—big deal.

The TR5 is still a novelty item. A good TR4A with Weber carbs should be just as fast. This raises the question once again of restoration costs. Is the price of new fuel injection parts worth the effort? Probably not.

The TR5 isn't a real serious collector car. If you can find a TR5 it'll probably cost a little more than a good TR4A, but not a whole lot more. If you want a TR4 that's just a little different from the rest then the TR5 is probably the car for you. Whether or not you should pay a premium price is another matter. You will most assuredly pay an extra amount when the injection system needs repairing.

If the car has right hand drive, and you live in the United States, then you should pay a lot less for the car. As much as a right hand drive car might provide a few miles of fun they're really totally useless. After the novelty wears off, you're going to find passing to be quite a nuisance.

What we have is a Triumph that has some historical value and very little practical value. If you can get one for the right price, meaning less than the price of a good TR4, then buy it. Just plan on spending extra money for the injection system and IRS repairs. The real question is whether the novelty of a TR5 is really worth all of the extra parts aggravation?

TR5 PI

ENGINE
Type: 6-cylinder, in line, water cooled, cast iron block and cylinder head
Bore x Stroke: mm/inches: 74.7x95/2.94x3.74
Displacement: cc/cubic inches: 2498/152
Valve Operation: ohv, pushrod operation
Compression Ratio: 9.5:1
Carburetion: Lucas indirect fuel injection
BHP (mfr): 150 (net) at 5500rpm

CHASSIS & DRIVETRAIN
Transmission: 4-speed, optional overdrive
Axle Ratio: 3.45:1
Rear Suspension: independent rear suspension, coil springs, semitrailing arms, lever dampers
Front Suspension: independent front suspension, coil springs, telescopic shocks

GENERAL
Wheelbase: 88"
Overall Length: 153"
Track: Front: 49.75"
        Rear: 49"
Brakes: Front: 10.9" discs
         Rear: 9"x1¾" drums
Tire Size: 165HR-15 radial ply
Wheel Size: 4.5x15, wire wheels optional
Weight: 2,268 lbs.

PERFORMANCE
Acceleration: 0-30: 2.6 seconds, 0-60: 8.1 seconds
Top Speed: 117mph

The "interim" TR5PI. Today it may well be one of the best six-cylinder Triumphs to collect. The rarest of all TRs, it makes an excellent highway car. Best of all, the sheet metal parts are the same as on a TR4A and the engine parts are shared with the TR6. A rare car with easy to locate parts! *Plain English Archive.*

Chapter 10

TR250

This was the TR the United States got instead of the TR5. Actually it was almost called the TR4B. The TR4 was now an old car. The market for sports cars was changing and it was a time when only the strong would survive. The British auto industry was entering the period when it would all but disappear.

Cars were being asked to be "good citizens" and performance was declining. The TR250 added two more cylinders and 300cc, but only four more horsepower. If you think of the TR250 as merely an interim car you won't be led astray.

The TR250 was built for only one year. Triumph knew that something else was needed to replace the TR4, but the effort couldn't be completed by 1968. The TR250 was the best effort they could make under the circumstances.

By 1968 the English were no longer producing state of the art sports cars. The cars were quaint an-

Triumph promoted all the reflector tape by saying it was "merely a subtle touch by day and [glows] like white fire at night when struck by the headlights of another car."

Triumph tried to do a great deal with no money on the TR250. *Plain English Archive.*

The TR250 was similar to the TR4A externally, but a stripe was added to the front and ugly reflector tape to the convertible top. This is one car that really needs wire wheels, or even better, factory magnesium wheels. The English fad of the period was to use wheelcovers that looked like mag wheels. The 250 was really an interim car designed to boost the dealers' sales while everyone waited for the TR6. *Plain English Archive.*

tiques even when they were brand new. Here was a new Triumph that offered no real performance gain over the previous model. Adding insult to injury, the car looked just like a TR4 when it sat in your driveway.

In an effort to create the impression of a new model, Triumph put large, brightly colored racing stripes across the nose of the car, and strips of reflective tape on the convertible top. Even more insulating were the cheap-looking hubcaps, replete with fake lug nuts. The side trim and turn-signal repeaters remained from the TR4A, with the new racing stripe running directly through them. These were desperate times at Triumph.

The original quality of the TR250 was not even close to the earlier cars. The seat surfaces were now made of vinyl and the dashboard lost every bit of sparkle as federal law eliminated the bright instrument bezels. Ironically Mazda would bring these bright bezels back with the RX-7. During this time though everything on the Triumph dash became black and boring. The TR250 wasn't really modern, and at the same time it had none of the charm of

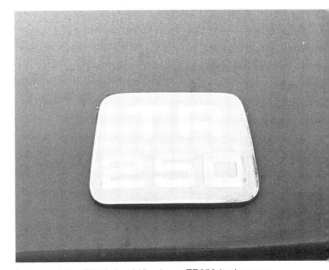

Instead of the TR4A "world," a large TR250 badge was placed on the left corner of the hood. The tops of the grille bars were painted black on the original TR250s to give a look of a new grille. *Bill Sohl photo.*

At the rear, two badges were used to highlight the model. Triumph named the car the TR250 to highlight the 2500cc displacement. It was also a way to save the 6 designation for the new car that was coming shortly. The TR250 also had back-up lights. *Bill Sohl photo.*

the older cars.

Even the big dashboard fresh-air outlets in the dash were dropped in favor of "eyeball" outlets that just wouldn't pass as much air as the older system. In general the interior of the TR250

A badge was also added to the side of the car, in the same location as the TR5 emblem. *Bill Sohl photo.*

was a step back from the TR4A.

The biggest problem with the TR250 is that the independent rear suspension became standard. If you take a TR250 on a rough road and hear a lot of banging and clanging prepare to spend some money. Also, crawl under the car and check to make sure that the frame mounts for the IRS aren't rusted. Everything that you would check for on a TR4A or TR6 should be closely examined on the TR250.

The engine is standard Triumph, even if it does have two more cylinders. The good part is that Triumph used carburetors on this car. They may give you problems but they certainly won't cost you as much money as the Lucas fuel injection system on the TR5.

The other point to consider is that Triumph offered some interesting options for the TR250. The eight spoke Minilite wheels are a nice addition. If you have to buy a set separate from the car you'll realize why they improve the value of a TR250. A common option today is to install Panasport wheels. They're slightly different from the Minilites, but they cost a lot less.

If you find a car with an original hardtop plan on paying a little extra, but this is money well

---

TR250

ENGINE
Type: 6-cylinder, in line, water cooled, cast iron block and cylinder head
Bore x Stroke: mm/inches: 74.7x95/2.94x3.74
Displacement: cc/cubic inches: 2498/152
Valve Operation: ohv, pushrod operation
Compression Ratio: 8.5:1
Carburetion: 2 Stromberg carburetors
BHP (mfr): 104 (net) at 4500rpm

CHASSIS & DRIVETRAIN
Transmission: 4-speed, optional overdrive
Axle Ratio: 3.7:1
Rear Suspension: independent rear suspension, coil springs, semitrailing arms, lever dampers
Front Suspension: independent front suspension, coil springs, telescopic shocks

GENERAL
Wheelbase: 88"
Overall Length: 153"
Track: Front: 49.25"
        Rear: 48.75"
Brakes: Front: 10.9" discs
         Rear: 9"x1¾" drums
Tire Size: 185-15 radial ply
Wheel Size: 5.0x15
Weight: 2,268 lbs.

PERFORMANCE
Acceleration: 0-30: 4.0 seconds, 0-60: 10.6 seconds
Top Speed: 107mph

spent. Remember, hardtops will extend your driving season by at least several months.

Despite all the problems with the TR250 there's a lot of interest in this car today. There are very few of the cars around and the TR250 has all the mechanical features of the TR6 with the TR4 body. Not a bad combination.

The TR250, while it will never be as popular as the TR6, is a good solid purchase. The only problem with the TR250 market is that the car is really not an improvement on the TR4A, and it's still not a TR6. Just make sure that you pay less for a nice TR250 than you would for a comparable TR6.

One of the few surviving original tops. The reflective strips were there so people would know that it was a TR250, not a TR4A. Not exactly the most dramatic idea, but one that fit both the introduction timetable and the budget. *Author collection.*

The TR250 dash with air conditioning installed: one of the nicest installations I've seen on a car of this period.

The Pioneer radio is obviously nonstandard. *Author collection.*

One of the rarest of all TR250s, with optional air. In the right-hand corner of the engine bay rests the air conditioning compressor. This was a dealer-installed option offered by Triumph, not an aftermarket kit. There are no figures as to how many TR250s got it. *Author collection.*

The owner of this car obviously feels strongly about the car. The exhaust pipes coming out from under the bumper are one sure way to tell a TR250 from a TR4A. *Author collection.*

This is the good wheel. If you find a set of the optional wheels in this condition prepare to pay serious money for them. It might be cheaper to just buy the whole car, es-pecially since the vintage racers have developed a fond-ness for these wheels. *Author collection.*

Chapter 11

★★★★ **Early cars**
★★★ **Later cars**

TR6

This is the one. The last of the great British roadsters. The TR6 was a throwback to another era. It was old when it was new. The design was an-cient, the car got lousy gas mileage, and it was never bolted together properly. In spite of all these problems, the TR6 came to be a car we all

All hardtops were designed by Les Moore and Triumph Styling. They're some of the nicest tops ever made and were designed to be a part of the car, not add-on accessories. A TR6 with the hardtop is one of the world's nicest GT cars. The TR6 body was reworked by Karmann, as Michelotti was too busy to take on the project. *Plain English Archive.*

This is one of the very earliest TR6s. It still has the mag-style wheelcovers and redline tires from the TR250. The switch to the later type wheel trim ring and open center was in answer to another request from the North American office. *Plain English Archive.*

love. After the demise of the Austin Healey 3000 this was the last big six-cylinder roadster left in production.

Not too many years ago you could get a TR6 really cheap. Then the TR6 market moved up a little bit. While prices have settled down don't ever look for a really cheap TR6. If you find one be prepared to own a worthless pile of junk.

The TR6 was produced from 1969 to 1977 and became the best-selling TR in history. About 92,000 examples of the TR6 were produced, 90 per cent of them built to United States specifications. This was the car that looked good, sounded right and could be pounded day after day.

As the last one rolled down the assembly line in July 1976, Phil Bott, who had worked at Triumph since 1953 said "It was full of character, beautifully streamlined." Canley Personnel Manager Dennis Hunt pointed out that "It rides hard and smells of oil. They just don't make cars like that anymore." A lot of Triumph collectors still agree with that thought.

You can't ignore the TR6. It'll leak oil in your driveway, the electrical system will drive you crazy and the rain will go right past all the window seals. But when the first warm day of Spring arrives you'll put the top down, your foot into the firewall and all those problems will seem minor.

The chassis and running gear of the TR6 was basically the same as that of the TR5/TR250. The big difference was the body. Fortunately Michelotti was too busy to work on a redesigned Triumph and the task was give to Karmann of Osnabruck, West Germany. He was previously known for his efforts with VW, Porsche and BMW.

Given only fourteen months, Karmann completely altered, and modernized, the TR4. He did all this keeping the TR4's cowl, doors and inner panels. You might think of what he did as a California custom job. He shaved off the superfluous hood bump, removed the chrome side trim and dumped the tubular grille. The rear was shaped into a sort of Kamm-back, painting the upright portion flat-black and wrapping the taillights horizontally.

Even though Triumph was never able to match the quality standards of the TR4, the TR6 was a semi-refined sports car. It featured carpeting on the floor as well as in the trunk. The seats looked a little better and the dash returned to a wood covering.

Mechanically a front anti-roll bar was added and the tire/wheel combination got a little wider. This was a remarkable facelift, achieved in record time, but it was still an evolution of the old TR4. When the car was introduced people had trouble understanding why they really needed the TR6.

Despite the total production numbers the TR6 never sold at the rate of the TR3 or the TR4. Nonetheless it was a steady, consistent seller which appealed to the traditional English car buyer. Indeed the TR6 did so well in the American market that when Triumph introduced a modern Triumph, the TR7, it was a disaster. For a lot of people the Triumph story ends with the TR6.

The car actually changed a great deal between 1969 and 1976. Most of the changes occurred to meet American safety and emissions regulations. The British had a great deal of difficulty meeting these regulations and the TR6 was diminished as a result of their attempts to conform to United States laws.

The worst blow was in 1971 when the compression was dropped from the original 8.5:1 to 7.5:1. The performance suffered accordingly. When the time came to meet the bumper height standards the total ride height was raised, just like the MGB, which had a real effect on handling.

Nineteen seventy-one was also the last year for wire wheels. Even though they look nice, wire wheels can involve a lot of time and effort to keep clean, not to mention round. The steel disc wheels of the later cars are a big improvement over the earliest examples, which kept the silly TR250 hubcaps. Unless you have a real fetish for wire wheels, and can afford to buy new wheels, stay away from the wire wheel TR6.

The appearance of the car didn't change as significantly as the performance, until 1973. That was the year Triumph decided to meet the bumper

The six-cylinder motor was carried over from the TR250. This means parts are fairly easy to come by for either car. The earliest TR6s used twin Strombergs. The air cleaner shown here is the stock version. The early versions of this motor put out 104hp at 4500rpm. *Author collection.*

The early TR6s all carried outline letters. This bit of art was inspired by the Pontiac GTO. The later cars carried the UK flag with a TR6 insert. All the graphics for Tri-umph, through the TR8, were done in the United States. *Author collection.*

regulations by putting huge rubber appendages on the bumpers. These can easily be removed today and the standard English bumper guards used to replace them.

These bumpers were the last change for the TR6. Fortunately Triumph was busy creating a TR7 and just left the TR6 alone. Given all the mistakes they made when they did try to change the car we were fortunate that they were too busy. The last TR6s were sold in the United States in 1977, and for that reason some may carry 1977 titles.

Rust is the major problem with the TR6, not just cosmetic rust but serious chassis rust, the sort that eats right through the frame. This is one reason that reproduction TR6 frames became available on the market several years ago. It's easier, and often cheaper, to just swap frames than attempting to repair a badly rusted example.

This frame deterioration usually begins at the rear of the chassis in the suspension mountings.

The body rust starts in the rocker panels and above the taillights. The factory applied undercoating breaks away from the sheet metal, forming a pocket for water accumulation. These pockets of undercoating never really dry out and before you know it you're into serious rust.

The best collector cars are the pre-1971 cars, provided they're in as good a condition as possible. The difference in price between a junker TR6 and a really nice TR6 is so small that you should never purchase a car needing major work. The carb models are far easier to work on than the fuel injection versions, which can aggravate the average do-it-yourself Triumph owner.

The real trick to being a happy TR6 owner is to avoid buying any example needing major repairs. Avoid all junk TR6s. A beaten TR6 will cost you a whole lot more money in the long run than what you would have paid for a ninety point show car. Another type of car to avoid is the one that's

The dash for the early TR6 remained the same as on the TR250. Things to look for are the black instrument bezels and small gauge needles that point down. The eyeball air vents were a mixed blessing compared to those used on the TR4. The correct finish for the dash on the TR6, as well as the TR250, is a dull finish, not high-gloss. *Author collection.*

just had a cosmetic restoration. A TR6 can be "patched up" rather inexpensively. These are the ones with a nice paint job, new seat covers and a worn out suspension. Don't pay for work that's simply going to have to be done all over again in the next twenty-four months.

The best TR6s can usually be found at Triumph meets and owned by members of Triumph clubs. These are generally the most well maintained examples. Enough TR6s have now been restored that you can wander around any Triumph gathering and look at a variety of examples.

It's doubtful if the TR6 will ever be a high-dollar car, but that's what makes it so interesting. You're not going to be driving an investment, you're going to be driving a car you enjoy. No one ever made money investing in Triumphs. Enthusiasts own them and if they can break even on all the parts they purchase over the years they're happy.

What you have with the TR6 is one of the best Triumphs ever made. This car, and the TR3, will be the cars that define Triumph for decades to come. Both cars will be the easiest to sell should you ever become bored and both are examples of why people enjoy Sunday drives in Triumphs.

TR6—FEDERAL VERSION

ENGINE
Type: 6-cylinder, in line, water cooled, cast iron cylinder block and head
Bore x Stroke: mm/inches: 74.7x95/2.94x3.74
Displacement: cc/cubic inches: 2498/152
Valve Operation: ohv, pushrod operation
Compression Ratio: 1969-1971: 8.5:1, 1972-1973: 7.75:1, 1974-1976: 7.5:1
Carburetion: 2 Stromberg 1.75 CD2 carburetors
BHP (mfr): 1969-1971: 104 (net) at 4500rpm, 1972-1973: 106 (net) at 4900rpm, 1974-1976: 106 (net) at 4900rpm

CHASSIS & DRIVETRAIN
Transmission: 4-speed, optional overdrive
Axle Ratio: 3.7:1
Rear Suspension: independent rear suspension, coil springs, semitrailing arms, lever dampers
Front Suspension: independent front suspension, coil springs, telescopic shocks

GENERAL
Wheelbase: 88"
Overall Length: 1969-1971: 159", 1972-1973: 162", 1974-1976: 163.6"
Track: Front: 49.25"
　　　Rear: 48.75"
Brakes: Front: 10.9" discs
　　　Rear: 9"x1¾" drums
Wheel Size: 5.5x15" steel disc, wire wheels optional on early cars
Tire Size: 165-15 radial ply
Weight: 1969-73: 2,390 lbs., 1974-76: 2,428 lbs.

PERFORMANCE (1969 model)
Acceleration: 0-30: 4.0 seconds, 0-60: 12.2 seconds
Top Speed: 109mph

Later in the life of the TR6 the small gauge needles were changed to point up. The steering wheel was also of a different design. In addition, all the little lights required by U.S. law began to appear on the dash. Most people like the early dash better. *Author collection.*

TR6—NON-FEDERAL VERSION

ENGINE
Type: 6-cylinder, in line, water cooled, cast iron cylinder block and head
Bore x Stroke: mm/inches: 74.7x95/2.94x3.74
Displacement: cc/cubic inches: 2498/152
Valve Operation: ohv, pushrod operation
Compression Ratio: 9.5:1
Carburetion: Lucas indirect fuel injection
BHP (mfr): 150 (net) at 5500rpm for the early cars, beginning with the CR series the horsepower was reduced to 124 bhp (din) at 5000rpm

CHASSIS & DRIVETRAIN
Transmission: 4-speed, optional overdrive
Axle Ratio: 3.7:1
Rear Suspension: independent rear suspension, coil springs, semitrailing arms, lever dampers
Front Suspension: independent front suspension, coil springs, telescopic shocks

GENERAL
Wheelbase: 88"
Overall Length: 159"
Track: Front: 49.25"
      Rear: 48.75"
Brakes: Front: 10.9" discs
      Rear: 9"x1¾" drums
Wheel Size: 5.5x15" steel disc, wire wheels optional on early cars
Tire Size: 165-15 radial ply
Weight: 2,473 lbs.

The rear of the TR6 was designed by Karmann but the idea for the flat-black paint was from Triumph North America. One suggestion that never made it to production was to use even larger taillights. *Author collection.*

On the later cars, the Triumph badge was moved to below the bumper. *Author collection.*

The 1971 front end is generally regarded as the nicest looking. The bumper was actually lower than on the pre- vious cars—note the distance between the lights and the top of the bumper. *Author collection.*

This is the front of a 1976 model. The big rubber bumpers are the most noticeable thing, and the parking lights have been moved to below the bumper. The spoil- er is something that was added when all the other little items were changed in 1974. *Author collection.*

Overdrive is not as common on the TR6 as it was on The earlier TRs, but it became standard with the 1974 Ameri- can-specification TR6. It's a nice option to have on your car, especially if you intend to use your TR6 for weekend trips. *Author collection.*

The headrests came in two different styles on the TR6. This is the later adjustable mode. The few cars that remained in England didn't get either version. Obviously the English saw no need for this additional American regulation. *Author collection.*

Chapter 12

TR7

This was the car that marked the end of Triumph. The car was so bad that no company could ever recover from this mistake. Just when they had a nice old English sports car in the TR6, Triumph decided to go modern. The TR7 is testimony that the English auto industry had no idea what they were doing.

This "flying doorstop" was designed for the American market and was a mistake right from the beginning. The design came from Austin in Longbridge, not Canley. The designer admitted that he'd only sketched a "doodle" which some insulated manager picked up and ran with.

This was the big change in TRs. Triumph planned on dropping the TR6 to make way for the all-new TR7. Both cars were offered for a short time before TR6 sales ended. The development of the TR6 was a slow, evolutionary process from the first TR2. The TR7 was the whole thing in one giant step. *Plain English Archive.*

Ghost view of the TR7 shows all. The outline TR7 lettering indicated cars that were built at the Speke works, and those are cars to avoid—quality is totally lacking. *Plain English Archive.*

The TR7 amounted to a slightly sporty sedan. An early decision was not to build a convertible. During the early design stages the Americans had not yet decided on new regulations for roll over protection. Perhaps, if the convertible had been introduced on the very first day America might have had a different reaction.

Triumph dealers had been asking for a new car for some time. They wanted a simple, reliable, and durable Triumph, the sort of car that built the Triumph reputation. What they got was a car that was not simple, unreliable, and anything but durable. This car was a shock to the loyal TR customer.

The TR7 suffered from the usual Triumph problems, as well as many that were brand new. For instance, if you find a TR7 that runs unevenly and overheats, check the compression. You probably have a blown headgasket. This is a common TR7 problem. If you're lucky you'll find it before you warp the cylinder head. This repair alone may cost more than the value of the car. Triumph cylinder heads do not come cheap—TR7s do.

The electrical systems on English cars have always been a problem but even here the TR7 set new standards. A lot of the early TR7s ran around with only one headlight—either to a failure of a motor or a water leak. The wiring system was modern, quite complex, and being British, was quite a tangled mess.

The original four-speed transmission, borrowed from the Austin Marina, proved to be especially weak and the second gear synchromesh was usually the first item to fail. Any TR7 with a four-speed should be avoided on general principles since the five-speed was far more flexible, not to mention more durable.

Even better advice is to avoid any TR7 with an ACG prefix on the serial number. All these cars were built at the infamous Speke plant near Liverpool, and suffered from an array of ailments that would fill this entire book. Leyland closed the

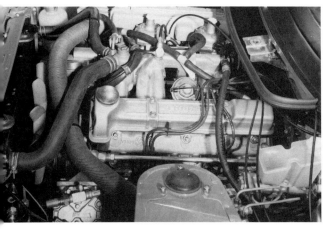 

The first American versions of the TR7 got a pair of Zenith-Stromberg 175 CD SEV carburetors, unless you bought the car in California. If you did that, then you got stuck with a single carburetor. Later cars got a fuel injection system. Both engine bays came with several yards of rubber hose. This was sign of the times. The typical TR7 engine has gone through a period of abuse, so be careful. If these engines are carefully maintained they can be very reliable. The only problem seems to be that the cylinder heads warp easily. If the car should ever overheat shut it off as soon as possible. *Plain English Archive & Author collection.*

TR7—NON-FEDERAL VERSION
ENGINE
Type: 4-cylinder, in line, water cooled, inclined at 45 degrees
Bore x Stroke: mm/inches: 90.3x78/3.56x3.07
Displacement: cc/cubic inches: 1998/122
Valve Operation: single overhead camshaft, chain driven
Compression Ratio: 9.25:1
Carburetion: 2 SU HS6 carburetors
BHP (mfr): 105 (din) at 5500rpm
CHASSIS & DRIVETRAIN
Transmission: 4-speed manual, overdrive not available; 5-speed manual optional; Borg-Warner-type automatic optional
Axle Ratio: 3.63:1
Front Suspension: independent front suspension, coil springs, McPherson struts
Rear Suspension: live axle, coil springs, radius arms
GENERAL
Wheelbase: 85"
Overall Length: 164.5"
Track: Front: 55.5"
     Rear: 55.3"
Brakes: Front: 9.7" discs
     Rear: 9"x1.75" drums
Tire Size: 185/70-13 or 175-13
Weight: 2,241 lbs., 2,355 lbs. with 5-speed equipment
PERFORMANCE
Acceleration: 0-30: 3.2 seconds, 0-60: 9.1 seconds
Top Speed: 109mph

TR7—FEDERAL VERSION
ENGINE
Type: 4-cylinder, in line, water cooled, inclined at 45 degrees
Bore x Stroke: mm/inches: 90.3x78/3.56x3.07
Displacement: cc/cubic inches: 1998/122
Valve Operation: single overhead camshaft, chain driven
Compression Ratio: 8.0:1
Carburetion: 2 Stromberg 175 CD SEV carburetors
BHP (mfr): 90 (din) at 5000rpm
CHASSIS & DRIVETRAIN
Transmission: 4-speed manual, overdrive not available; 5-speed manual optional; Borg-Warner-type automatic optional
Axle Ratio: 3.63:1
Front Suspension: independent front suspension, coil springs, McPherson struts
Rear Suspension: live axle, coil springs, radius arms
GENERAL
Wheelbase: 85"
Overall Length: 164.5"
Track: Front: 55.5"
     Rear: 55.3"
Brakes: Front: 9.7" discs
     Rear: 9"x1.75" drums
Tire Size: 175/70-13 or 175-13
Wheel Size: 5½-13
Weight: 2,241 lbs., 2,355 lbs. with 5-speed equipment
PERFORMANCE
Acceleration: 0-30: 4.3 seconds, 0-60: 11.3 seconds
Top Speed: 110mph

Speke plant, but not before it had destroyed what little remained of Triumph's reputation.

Road & Track did an early owner's survey for the TR7. Forty percent of the owners were unhappy with the general reliability of the car. Twenty-five percent were unhappy with the noise level, and fully a third of the owners had trouble with the headlights.

If you have the impression that you shouldn't buy a TR7 as a collector car, you're right. The TR7 should never be though, of as an investment. Some people like the shape of the car. If that's the case then buy a convertible.

Convertibles have always had a lot of appeal, and the TR7 is no exception. There were even two special edition models, the Spider and the Victory Edition. These were special trim editions that may be slightly more valuable than the regular convertibles.

A TR7 convertible is actually a nice car. If you find one of the later cars you'll actually enjoy driving the TR7. Just remember that the price has to be right, and the car should be in excellent shape. A junk TR7 will never be worth the value of the scrap steel. Buy the best convertible you can afford and enjoy it on the weekends.

One overlooked feature in all of this was the handling of the TR7. This was one thing the car did rather well. The car can pull 0.743g on the skidpad, compared to 0.680 for the TR6. This might make it a fun autocross car, but little more.

The TR7 was the end of Triumph. From the drawing board to the showroom floor the car was a mistake. There's really no reason to collect the car for future generations to own. The best reason to own a TR7 is because it's cheap. You can buy these cars for a fraction of what any other Triumph is going to cost. Just remember there's a reason for this low price.

The Triumph Spider was a special edition dressed in black with dual red pinstripes along the sides of the car. Spider lettering was added to the rear deck lid both sides. This was the first use of the alloy wheels that would become standard on the TR8. The Spider, or any

TR7 convertible is easily the best of the TR7s. The original TR7 logo, which can be seen on the nose of the car, was replaced with a Triumph wreath logo, which was later replaced by a metal and plastic raised badge. *Plain English Archive.*

The dash remained the same throughout the TR7 and TR8. The biggest problem with the interior was that the seats in early cars wore rapidly. The major difference was a changed tachometer in the TR8. *Plain English Archive.*

The later interior was a big improvement over the early cars. The problem in the future will be preservation of that huge plastic dash. If you plan on parking this car in the sun be sure to cover the dash. *Author collection.*

★ ★ ★

Chapter 13

TR8

The TR8 could have saved Triumph. The only problem was that by this time the British automotive industry had lost all imagination. They always seemed to be a about a week late, and several million dollars short. The TR8 stands as testimony to that singular fact. The TR8 had been developed at the same time as the TR7. There was only one problem. All the 3.5 engines had been

This is the best one. The TR8 Convertible is always going to be the most desired of the "wedge" shaped cars. Interest has been low, but it seems to be steadily increasing since production was stopped. Simply buy the best car you can possibly afford. Then maintain your new car in meticulous condition. I seriously doubt if anyone will ever do a ground up restoration on a TR8. It's just too complicated. *Author collection.*

The decals on the side and rear of the TR8 were designed in the United States. None of the British cars carried these decals. *Author collection.*

TR8—FEDERAL VERSION

ENGINE

Type: 90-degree V-8, aluminum block and heads, water cooled

Bore x Stroke: mm/inches: 89x71.1/3.5x2.8

Displacement: cc/cubic inches: 3528/215

Valve Operation: ohv, pushrod actuated

Compression Ratio: 8.1:1

Carburetion: 2 Stromberg Zenith 175 CDSET's, Lucas/Bosch fuel injection in California, all 1981 TR8's had fuel injection

BHP (mfr): 137 at 5000rpm, 148 at 5100rpm for fuel injection motors

CHASSIS & DRIVETRAIN

Transmission: 5-speed manual, Borg-Warner automatic optional

Axle Ratio: 3.08:1

Rear Suspension: live axle with sway bar

Front Suspension: independent MacPherson strut

GENERAL

Wheelbase: 85"

Overall Length: 165.5"

Track: Front: 55.5"
        Rear: 55.3"

Brakes: Front: 9.8" discs
         Rear: 9"x1.8" drums

Wheel Size: 5.5-13 cast alloy

Tire Size: 185/70-13 radials

Weight: 2,662 lbs., 2,650 lbs. with fuel injection

PERFORMANCE

Acceleration: 0-30: 2.9 seconds, 0-60: 8.4 seconds

Top Speed: 120mph

promised to Rover for the 3500 sedan.

The TR8 and the TR7 are really two quite different cars. They differ vastly in appeal. Americans could have been excited about a two-seater convertible powered by a V8. This car could have been the British Corvette. It would have packed people into the showrooms, and a lot of these people would have written checks for the TR8.

The problems in the British auto industry were too far advanced when the TR7, and the TR8, arrived. Triumph was in bad shape when the TR7s hit the dealers. The TR7 coupe only made it worse. By the time the TR8s arrived it was really too late. The TR8 was the end of the British car in America.

Nevertheless, the TR8 deserves a second look by collectors. The car is very similar to the Sunbeam Tiger. Everybody's been predicting great things about the value of these two cars for several decades now. Nothing has happened. The TR8 just hangs in there, keeping slightly ahead of inflation.

For all the good things that you can say about both the Tiger and the TR8, collectors have never flocked to either of the cars. The TR8 is a very nice car to drive and the people who own them love them. The problem is that not very many people even think about them.

Road & Track, in a typical moment of editorial glee, said that the TR8 could run away from anything on the road. The car could accelerate from 0-60mph in 8.4 seconds. Not exactly a rocket ship but respectable. The TR8 was slower than the

A long way from the TR2 engine! It's also one of the reasons that very few of these cars will ever be restored. They will either be carefully maintained or destroyed over time. It is always possible to assemble a basket-case TR3, but to attempt a similar TR8 restoration is inconceivable. *Bill Sohl photo.*

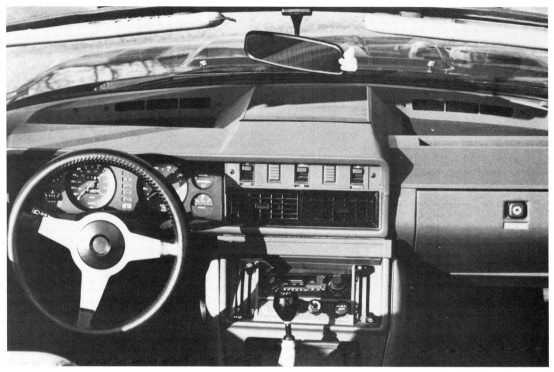

Even the dash is complicated. Very little of the old "pull out the instrument and replace it some afternoon" approach is possible with the TR8. The steering wheel was one change Triumph made with the TR8 and it did wonders for the appearance of the cockpit. *Bill Sohl photo.*

Corvette but it was still three seconds faster to 60mph than the TR7.

John Buffum, of rally fame, and under contract to Triumph, pointed out that "It handled similarly to all TRs. There's some initial understeer that you can balance by tipping on and off the throttle. Play the throttle and steering wheel together, and it'll go where you want." You can do that with a TR3 as well, you just do it faster with a TR8.

The standard collector's rule, often applied to a series of cars, is to buy either the very early models, or the very last ones. The early cars have value for their status as pioneers, the later ones for the perfection of a theme. There were so few TR8s produced that this rule seems almost silly. Fewer than 3,000 cars were manufactured and fewer than eighteen were made for the English market.

1978 coupes: 88 (78 to USA)
1979 coupes: 155 (124 to USA)
1980 coupes: 167 (158 to USA)
1980 convertibles : 2,006 (1,870 to USA)
1981 convertibles: 81 (78 to USA)

In contrast to the TR7, where the convertible is the rarer car, the rarer of the TR8s is the coupe. In 1981 there were no closed cars produced at all. The 1980 coupe is the rarest of all the TR8 models, but whether this will ever make up for the fun of the open cars is doubtful.

If somebody offers you a 1978 TR8 don't think that you're being sold an underwater ranch. These cars actually exist. Jaguar-Rover-Triumph brought the cars into the United States for a field test, after which they were sold to friends and associates. All were coupes, and most had automatic transmissions.

The big difference between the 1980 and the 1981 models is in the fuel injection. By 1981 all the TR8s had fuel injection, where previously, in 1980, only the California cars were so equipped. The rest of the world got Strombergs in 1980.

The biggest problem with the TR8 was that it looked just like a TR7. Rootes Motors had made the same mistake with the Sunbeam Tiger and the Sunbeam Alpine in the prior decade. Too bad the Triumph management hadn't paid attention. On the positive side though, this made it easier for TR8 owners to get parts.

Most of the TR8s currently on the market seem to have been well cared for. This was one car that was considered a collector car from the very first day. The original owners knew that this was the end of Triumph and that they were purchasing a car that would generate future interest.

If you do happen to find an abused TR8 simply walk away from the car. There is no sense in purchasing a beaten TR8. The value of a properly maintained car is so low that you really can't justify spending a great deal of money on these cars.

The reputation of the TR7 was what really ended the TR8. The cars were strange looking, and the prices were out of line with other cars in the market. The RX-7 was a much better buy at the time, and Mazda had a much better reputation for quality products.

The shame may have been that the TR8 was the right car at the wrong time. Maybe it was even the wrong company. That doesn't mean that it's a bad car, it just means that the TR8 will never reach the popularity of a good TR3.

TR8—NON-FEDERAL VERSION

ENGINE
Type: 90-degree V-8, aluminum block and heads, water cooled
Bore x Stroke: mm/inches: 89x71.1/3.5x2.8
Displacement: cc/cubic inches: 3528/215
Valve Operation: ohv, pushrod actuated
Compression Ratio: 8.1:1
Carburetion: 2 SU HIF6s
BHP (mfr): 165 at 5000rpm

CHASSIS & DRIVETRAIN
Transmission: 5-speed manual, Borg-Warner automatic optional
Axle Ratio: 3.08:1
Rear Suspension: live axle with sway bar
Front Suspension: independent MacPherson strut

GENERAL
Wheelbase: 85"
Overall Length: 165.5"
Track: Front: 55.5"
 Rear: 55.3"
Brakes: Front: 9.7" discs
 Rear: 9"x1.8" drums
Wheel Size: 5.5-13 cast alloy
Tire Size: 185/70-12 radials
Weight: 2,662 lbs.

The 1978 versions, as well as the 1980s and 1981s, all used the same wheels. These were far nicer than those that came on the early TR7s. *Author collection.*

The interior of the 1978 (top) was very similar to production models (bottom). *Author collection.*

The markings on the trunk were also designed in the United States but the cars on both sides of the ocean carried them. Just in case you miss the badges, the two exhaust pipes should give you a hint that this is no TR7. *Bill Sohl photo.*

These are the mystery cars; the 1978 TR8s. They were brought into the United States to serve as test cars and carried no markings. They were then sold to a limited group of Triumph associates. There are several differences between these cars and the later 1980 version that was sold to the general public. *Author collection.*

One difference on the '78 was the way the battery was situated in the trunk (top). The production version was out in the open. *Author collection.*

Chapter 14

Spitfire Mk 1

This is probably the rarest of all the mass-produced Triumphs. They made a bunch of these cars and they all rusted into the ground. Only four of the Mk I Spitfires exist in England and I'm willing to bet that there are less than fifty in the United States.

The Spitfire set new standards for inexpensive sports cars and quickly proved to be a real alternative to the previously dominant Austin-Healey

The Mk 1 GT was the best looking of all the Spitfires. The hardtop was offered for the first time in the Fall of 1963 and continued until the introduction of the Mk IV. They are easily identifiable in flea markets and unlike the cars, the hardtops didn't rust! At this point there may well be more Mk 1 hardtops than there are complete cars. *Plain English Archive.*

Here's the American version of the early Spitfire. Except for the full hubcaps and the amber parking lights, the cars were the same. Only the position of the steering wheel and the associated controls varied. This particular car started its life as a right-hand drive, was converted to left-hand drive, and later converted back to right-hand drive for rallying use. *Plain English Archive.*

Sprite. Contrary to what the management at Leyland thought, you could have fun in a cheap sports car with roll-up windows. You even got independent suspension in your Triumph Spitfire, although not a really good one, for less than the price of an MGB.

Most of the parts came from the Triumph Herald, but parts borrowing had long been a feature of cheap sports cars, so who really cared? The Triumph Spitfire was a lot of fun for very little money.

The technology of the Triumph Herald dictated most of the mechanical specifications for the Spitfire. The engine received some small changes in valve timing and carburetion, which resulted in 63hp, as opposed to the Herald's 51hp. In order to get the seats in the Spitfire low enough the engineers moved the sides of the frame to the center of the car. This is usually called a backbone chassis. Lotus used a similar method with the Elan, introduced at about the same time.

The body shell was welded together (the Herald was bolted together). The sills, or rocker panels provided the body stiffness. These two facts are the reason that there are so few Spitfires around today.

Once these rocker panels, or sills, begin to rust, the body of the car becomes very flexible, and very expensive to repair. The Mk 1 Spitfires were

The Spitfire engine was basically the Triumph Herald 1200 engine. The carburetors were twin 1.25in SUs. A 9.0:1 compression ratio and a different camshaft raised the power from 39hp to 63hp (55 net hp). A good feature is that all the parts are easy to reach. *Author collection.*

SPITFIRE MK 1

ENGINE
Type: 4-cylinder, in line, water cooled
Bore x Stroke: mm/inches: 69.3x76/2.728x2.992
Displacement: cc/cubic inches: 1147/70
Valve Operation: ohv, pushrod operation
Compression Ratio: 9.0:1
Carburetion: 2 SU HS 2s
BHP (mfr): 63 at 5750rpm
CHASSIS & DRIVETRAIN
Transmission: 4-speed
Axle Ratio: 4.11:1
Rear Suspension: swing axle independent suspension, transverse leaf spring and radius rods
Front Suspension: independent front suspension, telescopic shocks
GENERAL
Wheelbase: 83"
Overall Length: 145"
Track: Front: 49"
        Rear: 48"
Brakes: Front: 9" discs
        Rear: 7"x1¼" drums
Tire Size: 5.20x13
Wheel Size: 3.5x13
Weight: 1,568 lbs.
PERFORMANCE
Acceleration: 0-30: 4.6 seconds, 0-60: 16.5 seconds
Top Speed: 92mph

really throw-away cars. Repairs to the body could easily exceed the value of the car. Keep in mind that plastic body putty does not restore the strength of welded panels.

The body shell was attached to the structural backbone at twelve different points. The tilting hood and front fenders were ideas borrowed from the Herald. This tilting front end made the engine and front suspension simple to work on.

The Spitfire package looked pretty good when compared to the rival Sprite. The Austin-Healey Sprite lacked both roll-up windows and a real trunk. The only thing in the Sprite's favor was that it had a real suspension at the back of the car—no small matter.

If you drove a Spitfire on the ragged edge, the inside wheel would tuck under the car and make your life very exciting. This wasn't a real problem because most people never drove the car fast enough to cause a problem. Nonetheless, it hurt the car's reputation.

The fix for this handling problem was to add a camber compensator to the rear axle. VW Beetle owners had been using this same technique for several years. This camber compensator eventually became a standard Triumph part. If you purchase an early Spitfire, and it doesn't have a camber compensator installed, get one. If you intend on impressing people with your driving ability at speed you'll need it.

The front suspension was so good that it became the standard for all the open wheel racing cars of the sixties. Spitfire front suspensions also found themselves on the front of the Lotus Europa and the Elan. The Triumph Spitfire and the Triumph Six front suspension probably did more for cheap formula car racing than any other factor in the sixties.

There wasn't anything particularly exotic about this suspension. It consisted of upper and lower a-frames, a telescopic shock and a coil spring. This simple front suspension was simply well designed and ruggedly built.

These early Spitfires were an instant success and usually outsold the Austin Healey Sprites and MG Midgets combined. (Actually, you should count the Sprite and Midget as one car, since it was really a case of different trim emblems placed on the same sports car. That's why the term "Spridget" was coined to describe the two cars.) The Spit-

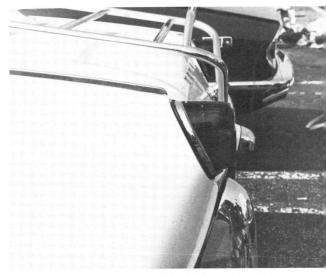

The taillights stayed the same until the Spitfire underwent the Triumph family treatment. The car behind the Mk 1 shows the change. *Author collection.*

A young Stirling Moss and Valerie Pirie are shown with what the factory would lead us to believe was a rally car. The car was an American-specification model with right-hand drive and amber parking lights. It would be fun to decide what the correct way to restore this car might be. *Plain English Archive.*

This is one of the few restored Mk 1 Spitfires. The use of the 4 in the car's badge led to endless speculation that there would soon be a six-cylinder Spitfire. The truth was that the 4 was included to differentiate the Spitfire from the Sports Six that was to be sold in the United States. The Sports Six was known as the Vitesse in England. *Author collection.*

fire was quite simply a more modern car. Today the table is reversed. Everyone wants a Bugeye Sprite and an early Mk I Spitfire is virtually impossible to find, but very few people seem to want an early Spitfire anyway.

There's very little collector interest in these cars, and most have simply rusted into the ground. No Spitfire will ever approach the value of a good Bugeye, or even a nice TR4. The Spitfire is one Triumph you'll probably never even break even on.

At the same time the car is a lot of fun to drive. We're talking low investment and high fun content. Buy it, drive it, and maintain it. You really shouldn't consider a full-blown restoration since the cost will be so far over the value of the car.

The cost of restoring a basket-case Spitfire will easily exceed the value of the car, by several factors. Spitfires are a nice car but they bring very little money. Buy it because you like it, not because you expect to make money, or even break even.

This has to be an American car, with a third type of wheel cover. The real question is whether the car is a Mk 1 or a Mk 2. *Plain English Archive.*

The steering wheel is not original and the shifting lever knob is an aftermarket option. Part of the fun of owning a Spitfire was, and still is, that the low cost left you with money for little things to be added to the car. Fortunately,

Spitfire concours judging hasn't reached the point where these things are held against the car. The fun of the Spitfire is in making it your own. *Author collection.*

Just to keep everyone confused, here's another American car with left-hand drive and amber parking lamps.

The wheelcovers are the small variety but have wide trim rings installed (an early option). *Plain English Archive.*

Author collection.

★ ★

Chapter 15

Spitfire Mk 2

The Mk 2 Spitfire is a better buy than the Mk 1. First in a series counts for very little when there's almost no collector interest in a car. Secondly, the Mk 2 is simply a better car than the Mk 1. The Mk 2 has improved seats and more power. By this time the seats are usually worn out in both of the models but since the ones in the Mk 2 are a little lower the vision through the windshield is a little better.

The optional wire wheels are a full inch wider than the standard steel wheels, but the replacement cost for these wire wheels is going to be a whole lot more. Wire wheels are nice when they're new but over time the spokes loosen and the wheels go out of round. Whatever the wire wheels may have originally contributed to the overall handling has been lost through age. Good steel wheels are superior to twenty-five-year-old wire wheels.

The real reason to recommend the Mk 2 is that it has the improvements, without the add-on modifications, that the British used to meet American laws. After the Mk 2 the Spitfire became something the original designers never intended. The changes after the Mk 2 detracted from the original concept. Keep in mind though that there is really very little difference in Spitfires from beginning to end.

When cars became subject to a variety of American laws the British reacted by simply adding parts in an effort to meet the standards. The English never really liked the American market, even though they made most of their money in the United States. What happened was the graft-on modifications usually made the car look ugly, and the tacked on emissions devices made them run poorly. The British really didn't seem to care.

These facts all make the Mk 2 Spitfire a good car to own. When *Road & Track* and *Autocar* tested the Mk 1 and the Mk 2 there was no difference in the top speed of the two cars. The most interesting aspect though, was that one had overdrive and the other did not. This tells us one thing—at 92mph the Spitfire was flat out of horsepower—no changes in gearing could make a difference.

The bar running between the bumper guards was a dealer-installed, non-factory option. *Plain English Archive.*

The luxury version with full wheelcovers and whitewall tires. The Spitfire Mk 2 cost $2,199 in 1965. The hardtop was $100 extra. *Plain English Archive.*

SPITFIRE MK 2

ENGINE
Type: 4-cylinder, in line, water cooled
Bore x Stroke: mm/inches: 69.3x76/2.728x2.992
Displacement: cc/cubic inches: 1147/70
Valve Operation: ohv, pushrod operation
Compression Ratio: 9.0:1
Carburetion: 2 SU HS 2's
BHP (mfr): 67 at 6000rpm

CHASSIS & DRIVETRAIN
Transmission: 4-speed, optional overdrive
Axle Ratio: 4.11:1
Rear Suspension: swing axle independent suspension, transverse leaf spring and radius rods
Front Suspension: independent front suspension, telescopic shocks

GENERAL
Wheelbase: 83"
Overall Length: 145"
Track: Front: 49"
       Rear: 48"
Brakes: Front: 9" discs
        Rear: 7"x1¼" drums
Tire Size: 5.20x13
Wheel Size: 3.5x13
Weight: 1,568 lbs.

PERFORMANCE
Acceleration: 0-30: 4.2 seconds, 0-60: 15.0 seconds
Top Speed: 92mph

The Spitfire was a better car with all the factory options attached. The single best option was the hardtop. This really changed the car. What was previously an open leaky fun car now became something closer to a true GT car, as if that were possible with a Spitfire. The hardtop changed the interior sounds and the comfort level was a little higher. Most owners who have hardtops actually use them in the cooler seasons. That tells you all you need to know about the utility of the hardtop.

In early 1964 Triumph offered tuning kits that are virtually impossible to locate today. The Interim kit was the mildest and consisted of a downdraft Solex carb and different intake and exhaust manifolds. This really adds very little to the car and is mainly a conversation piece.

The Stage I kit was never actually distributed, nor built, so you can simply ignore that option. Stage II is so rare that you'll probably spend your entire life without ever seeing one. This was an eight-port cylinder head with twin DCOE Webers. In addition Triumph included a higher-lift camshaft and an exhaust header. This was the racing option.

If you really want more power, and who doesn't, the best program is to build your own engine from what's offered by the suppliers listed in the end of this book. Tuning technology has come a long way in the past thirty years, so why not make use of the advances, rather than searching out old parts.

Spitfires are great little cars for club racing, hillclimbs, and autocrosses. They're cheap, they're fun, and you aren't destroying some valuable piece of automotive history to have this fun. The engines are dead reliable and the technology is very basic.

The trick in buying a Spitfire is condition. This is the single most important item. Avoid junk Spitfires. The cost of putting a junk Spitfire in decent shape could easily be triple the cost of buying a decent one in the first place.

The advantage of buying a pre-1968 Spitfire is that there were no emission control devices installed. More and more states are requiring that all cars have original, and operating, emissions systems. They're checking to see that all the devices that the factory originally installed are present and functioning. If your car lacks these items you're denied registration.

There's a great deal to be said for buying one of these early Spitfires. For low buck fun the Mk 2 Spitfire is one of the best bargains around. You'll never make a lot of money with one of these early Spitfires, but on the other hand you won't spend a lot of money either. We're talking about having fun with this car.

Author collection.

115

★ ★ ★

Chapter 16

Spitfire Mk 3

The goal with the Mk 3 was to be able to legally import the car into the United States. The Mk 3 Spitfire was the first year that the car had to conform to the new American emissions and safety laws. This was the beginning of the end. Everyone had trouble with the new regulations. Porsche and Mercedes both produced some very bad cars during the same time period. The difference was that

The rear of the Spitfire Mk 3 was getting a little crowded with all the separate lights. Note that the 4 emblem was dropped with this model. The exhaust system is an after-market system—one outlet per cylinder. This is an owner who likes the way his Spitfire sounds. *Author collection.*

One of the seldom-mentioned features of the Mk 3 Spitfire is that the electrical system was changed to negative-ground. This means that all of the electrical components are different. Some will work either way, but others will not. It's one more thing to confuse you while you scrounge the flea markets for parts. *Plain English Archive.*

the British never recovered from their mistakes.

The good part of the Mk 3 Spitfire was that Triumph made a few changes that actually improved the car. In fact, it had the best engine of the entire Spitfire line. One possible change would be to transplant this Spitfire Mk 3 1296cc engine into a Mk 2 car. This could be the best of all possible worlds.

This new 1296cc motor was similar to the motor found in the Triumph 1300 sedan and a few racing cars. The cylinder head was an eight-port version with each valve getting its very own passage. This also meant that the cylinder head wouldn't fit on the earlier engine blocks. The good part is that there is nothing to prevent you from simply dropping an entire engine into an earlier Spitfire.

The only emissions equipment found on the Mk 3 was a PCV valve. This valve should be on the top of the intake manifold, just above the rear carburetor. This was probably removed several years ago by some owner who thought that removing emissions devices would improve the performance of the car. It didn't make any improvement and now you'll have to locate a replacement. This isn't a big deal, just some small aggravation.

It was the bumpers though that really signaled the change. The bumper was raised to the middle of the grille. The Spitfire would never really look the same again. Except for the appearance, the Mk 3 Spitfire may be the best of the bunch.

The brakes were improved slightly as well. Triumph installed larger discs on the front of the car. Just to prove they were modern, Triumph installed gas shocks in the rear. This fact is of absolutely no significance to anyone purchasing a twenty-five-year-old Spitfire today.

Car and Driver continued to complain about the handling: "Drive hard and the car skitters sideways more like a family sedan than a true sports car." The reality is that the average Spitfire owner only drives this fast about once a year. This is a fun car to drive, not a race car, something the car magazines seemed to forget.

The interior of the Mk 3 was the best of all possible worlds. There was a quaint walnut veneer finish around the instruments. Where the previous dashes had painted surfaces the Mk 3 had vinyl.

From 1970 on, the Mk 3 used a single Zenith-Stromberg carburetor in the United States. The engine retained the camshaft profile from the Mk 2, but changed the exhaust manifold. The cylinder head had eight ports, where the Mk 1 and 2 cars used six. If you're going to swap engines around in early Spitfires, this is one of the best, especially with dual carburetors. *Author collection.*

The original carpeting, which has long since worn out, was of a better quality. Triumph even went so far as to install mounting points for shoulder harnesses. However, they never did get around to putting in the actual shoulder harnesses.

Triumph even decided that it was time to install a permanent convertible top. The days of assembling the top like a kit were over. Today I would actually prefer the kit because you can leave it home when you don't need it. Remember very few Spitfires are used for daily transportation.

Since there are very few early Spitfires driving around, these Mk 3s have taken on a new popularity. They, and the Spitfire 1500, are the survivors.

They're not a bad purchase and offer a lot of fun. Just as with all other Triumphs avoid any car that needs serious work. Buy one where somebody else has spent all the money. This will make it a lot easier to enjoy the car.

The Spitfire used 13in 60-spoke wire wheels. The wheels are interchangeable between different cars. Also, if you're really set on converting to wire wheels, try to find an older car in the junkyard and swap the appropriate suspension pieces around. It's much less expensive than buying new parts, or even trading cars. *Plain English Archive.*

★★★

Chapter 17

Spitfire Mk IV

The Mk IV was really a continuation of the Mk 3. The Spitfire was moving even further from the concept of a cheap basic sports car. The British were still attempting, with little success, to deal with the American laws on emissions and safety standards. The American standards were getting tougher and the English weren't doing any better than they had done with the Mk 3.

The Mk IV used a new front hood without the metal ridges where the fenders met the hood panel. The wheels, which looked very much like those on the TR6, were also installed to give the car a Triumph family look. *Plain English Archive.*

This is one car that's easy to identify. The new rear-end design was applied to the whole Triumph family. *Author collection.*

The really big difference with the Mk IV was the rear styling of the car. The tail of the car was given the Kamm treatment. The Spitfire would now resemble all the other Triumphs and a new full-width bumper was added. The down-side was the addition of two huge rubber blocks to the front of the car. While every car manufacturer in the world was having trouble with the new American safety standards it somehow seemed the English went out of their way to insult the American market.

The mechanical changes were an improvement. The greatest mechanical transformation consisted of an all-synchro transmission and a new rear suspension. With this new axle the transverse rear spring was allowed to pivot on top of the differential casing. This reduced the rear roll stiffness and minimized the rear wheel camber changes.

The overdrive was still an option, while the complaints about narrow tires were answered by making 4 1/2in wheels standard. In today's world that isn't a great deal. Nonetheless you should remember these Spitfires are about fun, not high performance at the limit.

The transmission transformation is the one you'll find the most worthwhile. Driving in today's traffic the all-synchro transmission is a lot more fun than the earlier gearboxes. The only problem is that this transmission was coupled with a new rear axle ratio, 3.98 versus the earlier 4.11. This gives you a little less acceleration.

The real decline in acceleration comes from dropping the horsepower back to 63hp, from the earlier 75hp. The main reason for this was the need to conform to American emissions standards. When brand new, the Mk IV was about a full second slower to 60mph than the previous Mk 3. Keep in mind that when we talk about twenty-five-year-old cars that's not a big deal.

The car magazines of the era began to loose interest in the Spitfires and call the whole package archaic. They viewed it as a holdover and a car that had no real purpose. To many it seemed like a pseudo luxury car, built to a price, and then not put together very well at all.

Today you need to consider whether you should jump directly to the later Spitfire 1500, or

The Mk IV dash was carried over into the 1500 series. This particular dash is from the 1973 model. *Plain English Archive.*

SPITFIRE MK IV

ENGINE
Type: 4-cylinder, in line, water cooled, cast iron block, cast iron head
Bore x Stroke: mm/inches: 74x76/2.90x2.99
Displacement: cc/cubic inches: 1296/79.2
Valve Operation: ohv, pushrod/rocker arm
Compression Ratio: 9.0:1
Carburetion: Twin SU HS2s, single 1.50 CDSE Zenith Stromberg on federal version
BHP (mfr): 75 at 6000rpm; 58 at 5200rpm, federal; 48 at 5500rpm, 1972 federal

CHASSIS & DRIVETRAIN
Transmission: 4-speed, overdrive optional on 3rd top gear
Rear Suspension: independent, swing axle, transverse leaf spring with radius rods and pivoting-spring location
Axle Ratio: 3.89:1
Front Suspension: independent, A-arms, coil springs, telescopic shocks

GENERAL
Wheelbase: 83"
Overall Length: 149"
Track: Front: 49"
      Rear: 48"
Brakes: Front: 9.0" discs
      Rear: 7.0"x1.25" drums
Wheel Size: 4.5x13 steel disc wheel, wire wheels optional
Tire Size: 145 SR 13
Weight: 1,717 lbs.

PERFORMANCE
Acceleration: 0-30: 4.2 seconds, 0-60: 14.4 seconds
Top Speed: 98mph

buy one of the early cars that seem to be just a little more frivolous and more fun. The Mk IV was an attempt at mass class that didn't work very well.

One reason to consider the Mk IV Spitfire is for the improved interior. The Mk IV interior was based on the appointments in the GT6, which was an advancement over the earlier Spitfires. The gauges were moved over in front of the driver and the heater controls were a little more refined. In addition you get a nicer steering wheel.

The only reason to buy a Mk IV Spitfire is because you've located a really nice example at a low price. If you buy this type of car you can have a lot of fun. If you get an example that needs a lot of work then you're probably throwing money down a black hole. If you're intent on getting a Mk IV Spitfire then try to find one built prior to 1971. In 1971 the horsepower dropped down to 58 net horsepower, and even this declined to 48 in 1972. Even worse, these engines suffered greater torque losses, which is really what we feel when we push down on the accelerator. Things were getting so bad that the English rushed the 1500 engine into the United States Spitfires during the end of 1973. Even the English were getting embarrassed by the lack of power.

The Mk IV kept the same front suspension as the earlier cars. You can notice the new alternator directly in front of the ignition coil. *Author collection.*

Not only did the Mk IV get a new body design, but it got a new hardtop design as well. Triumph seemed to be on a roll with hardtops. This one, just like the TR6, improves the styling of the car. *Plain English Archive.*

This was the last Spitfire that used a single circuit brake system. The cylinder in the foreground is the clutch master cylinder, and the brake cylinder is the one in the rear of the picture, just like the pedals. If you get these confused in your parts pile, and install them in the wrong location you're going to have a problem. Only the outside of the cylinders is the same. *Author collection.*

★★★

Chapter 18

Spitfire 1500

This was the last one. This final series of Spitfires was introduced in the fall of 1973, as a 1974 model. The price was $2,895, up about $700 from ten years before. Before the final Spitfire was sold in 1980 the price would rise to $7,365. This was an outlandish price to pay for a small sports car, and the sales figures reflected that one simple fact.

On the other hand this final Spitfire is the most comfortable and best handling Spitfire of the bunch. In a moment of editorial excess *Road & Track* compared it to the Lotus Elan. *Car and Driver* found it superior to the MGB and MG Midget, which may have been true but that still doesn't make it a good car. The rest of the automobile in-

The engine in the Spitfire 1500 used a single Zenith-Stromberg CD4 carburetor. The factory quoted 57hp for this engine, but somehow it never felt like all 57 were working at the same time. But with a 7.5:1 compression ratio it can easily be run on today's lousy gasoline. *Author collection.*

Most Spitfire 1500s used a decal for identification, but this car is shown with a metal badge. This was only done on the 1974 cars. Notice how much larger the rubber bumpers became in 1974. Also, take note of the new front spoiler. *Plain English Archive.*

dustry had long since gone beyond MG. Using the last of the MGBs as a benchmark is not a good comparison.

The 1500 is the easiest Spitfire to drive, as well as the most comfortable. It lacks the acceleration of the earliest Spitfires but with better low-end torque you simply don't notice the difference in power. The engine still makes more noise than any modern day small car but then again nobody purchases Spitfires for their sophistication.

The old 1296cc engine had reached the end of the journey. The Spitfire was down below 48hp. The 1972 car had the least power of all the Spitfires ever built. The top speed was down below 80mph, and nothing could be done to improve the situation.

The British didn't get this final Spitfire until December of 1974, but then again they really didn't need the larger engine. The English Mk IV was developing an adequate 75hp. When they finally did get the 1500 engine they were a little surprised that it only had 71hp. That may have been a lot more than the Americans got, but still less than they were used to having. The big difference between

the horsepower ratings in the two countries was that the English cars could use the twin SU carbs while the Americans got the single Zenith-Stromberg CD4, plus an air pump. In California the 1500 even had a catalytic converter.

The real question is whether the car deserves any special attention at this point in history. There's no dramatic difference over the earlier cars, nor is it especially unique. The 1500 is definitely more comfortable than a Mk 1, but that's missing the point. The early cars may be a little crude, but they can be a little more fun.

The 1500 Spitfire was really a patchwork response to American emission and safety standards. When the Spitfire 1500 was new it was unreliable, poorly assembled and started to rust the second week you owned the car. Leyland had given up on the Spitfire. They were too busy working on the new TR7 to be bothered with this old sportscar.

The 1500 changed only in response to the laws, not the marketplace. There was no effort to make the Spitfire a better car. By 1976 the factory even gave up listing horsepower. Once you get

SPITFIRE 1500—NON-FEDERAL VERSION

ENGINE
Type: 4-cylinder, in line, water cooled, cast iron block, cast iron head
Bore x Stroke: mm/inches: 73.7x87.5/2.90x3.44
Displacement: cc/cubic inches: 1500/91.1
Valve Operation: ohv, pushrod/rocker arm
Compression Ratio: 9.0:1
Carburetion: 2 SUs
BHP (mfr): 71 at 5500rpm

CHASSIS & DRIVETRAIN
Transmission: 4-speed, optional overdrive on top gear
Axle Ratio: 3.89:1, 2.90 with optional overdrive
Rear Suspension: independent, swing axle, transverse leaf spring with radius rods and pivoting-spring location
Front Suspension: independent, A-arms, coil springs, telescopic shocks

GENERAL
Wheelbase: 83"
Overall Length: 149"
Track: Front: 49"
     Rear: 50"
Brakes: Front: 9.0" discs
     Rear: 7.0"x1.25" drums
Wheel Size: 4.5x13
Tire Size: 155 SR 13
Weight: 1,735 lbs.

PERFORMANCE
Acceleration: 0-30: 4.7 seconds, 0-60: 15.4 seconds
Top Speed: 98mph

This was the final dash arrangement for the Spitfire. Restoring the wood is an easy job, and usually a necessary one. *Author collection.*

below a certain level it makes little difference. Besides no one ever bought a Spitfire for the tremendous horsepower.

You might want to avoid any Spitfire with a catalytic converter since the price of this part is beyond the pale. A lot of states have started enforcing emissions laws to the point that all factory-installed emissions devices must be present, and operating. If you intend to drive the car you have to conform, no exceptions.

The evolution of the 1500 was in response to changing laws and a need to lower the manufacturing costs. There's nothing remarkable about the engineering of the 1500. Then again that's why the average hobbyist can work on the car. What was seen as a deficit in the mid-seventies is now an attribute.

Today the Spitfire can be purchased for very little money. The downside is that the parts, while readily available, are expensive given the car's low price. You own a Spitfire because you love it. Like all the loves of your life this one is going to cost you more money than you ever intended. That doesn't make it bad, it just means that occasionally you need to touch reality before you spend a lot of money on a Spitfire.

Today the 1500 Spitfire is a better car to own than the MG Midget, and a lot easier to work on than a Fiat X1/9. Both cars were initially superior but times have changed. The Fiat, while technically superior, is far more difficult to work on and the parts are simply not available.

One good reason to purchase an earlier Spitfire, as opposed to the 1500, is to avoid the clumsy attempts to meet American emissions standards. There's very little, if any, emissions equipment for the state inspectors to get excited about on the earlier cars.

The trade off with the earlier cars is that you get a poorer rear suspension system and a less comfortable interior. What it comes down to in the end is, "What choices are in the marketplace?" Any Spitfire in good condition, at the right price, is a better buy than a rolling basket case. You can argue all the nuances of the various Spitfires but condition is the single most important criterion, not the specific model.

In spite of all the negative points a mechanically sound Spitfire 1500 can be a lot of fun to own. It's possibly the best of the bunch. At the very least it's a pleasant little car that can provide you with some lovely Sunday afternoons in the country. When we evaluate it as a car the Spitfire it's lacking in a lot of respects. If you look at it as an entertainment device it's a lot more fun than computer games—at least on nice Spring days.

The tilting hood remained a Spitfire feature right to the end. The way to own a flawless 1500 like this one is to buy the finest car on the market. Then carefully go over every square inch of the car. Doing a ground-up restoration on a poor example makes little or no sense. Some of the Spitfire 1500s have already gotten to the point where they're worth very little. Avoid those cars and go for the best example. *Author collection.*

SPITFIRE 1500—FEDERAL VERSION

ENGINE
Type: 4-cylinder, in line, water cooled, cast iron block, cast iron head
Bore x Stroke: mm/inches: 73.7x87.5/2.90x3.44
Displacement: cc/cubic inches: 1500/91.9
Valve Operation: ohv, pushrod/rocker arm
Compression Ratio: 7.5:1
Carburetion: Single Stromberg CD4
BHP (mfr): 57 at 5000rpm

CHASSIS & DRIVETRAIN
Transmission: 4-speed, optional overdrive on top gear
Axle Ratio: 3.89:1, 2.90 with optional overdrive
Rear Suspension: independent, swing axle, transverse leaf spring with radius rods and pivoting-spring location
Front Suspension: independent, A-arms, coil springs, telescopic shocks

GENERAL
Wheelbase: 83"
Overall Length: 149"
Track: Front: 49"
        Rear: 50"
Brakes: Front: 9.0" discs
          Rear: 7.0"x1.25" drums
Wheel Size: 4.5x13
Tire Size: 155 SR 13
Weight: 1,735 lbs.

These two photos show the difference between the Mk 3 engine (left) and the Spitfire 1500 (right). What makes this picture confusing is that the 1500 is a Canadian version of the Spitfire. They still got the dual SU carbs. In the United States we got the single Stromberg. We were allowed to have the alternator in the United States. *Author collection.*

It was almost as if Triumph couldn't put enough badges on the new 1500 Spitfire. They wanted to make sure that you knew this was a new model. *Author collection.*

This is the tandem brake cylinder used after commission number 4001. These aren't all that easy to rebuild in your home garage, but any number of people have done it successfully. While the price might seem cheap to Ferrari owners, most of us who have been around English cars for the last three decades find the cost a little high. If you're replacing or rebuilding a master cylinder then you should probably just keep going through the rest of the brake system. When you're all done fill the system with silicone brake fluid. *Author collection.*

Chapter 19

★★	GT6
★★	GT6+
★★	GT6 Mk 3

GT6

This was the car the Datsun 240Z killed. It was also one of the better Triumphs, if you can fit into the car. The GT6 was a derivative of the Spitfire, but instead of the four-cylinder Spitfire engine Triumph used a really nice revving, smooth six-cylinder engine. The combination of the Spitfire size and the six-cylinder engine resulted in a really pleasant little car. This GT6 was produced as an afterthought, not even Triumph knew where they were going to sell the car. It was a car Triumph made because they thought they could. The first prototype was built in 1963. The idea was that this was to be a mini E-Type. If Triumph had been a little better organized it might have been.

The real problem was that Triumph built a nice little car and never considered who might buy it. The GT6 was an engineering project without a marketing program. They were operating under the idea that if they built it then the customers would find it. It was a car with no customers.

Things haven't changed much since 1970 when the GT6 was introduced. The GT6 market is still limited to Triumph enthusiasts, especially those who already own some other Triumph products. For these Triumph enthusiasts the GT6 is an appealing car to own. The only problem is that, just like when it was new, there's not very much interest in the car. You not only have a limited interior, but you also have a limited market for these cars.

One early misconception about the GT6 was that it was derived from the competition Spitfire GT while exactly the opposite was true. The GT was designed around the Spitfire because it was cheaper to build than if it had been constructed around the TR6 chassis.

The magic number was $3,000. Triumph felt that if they stayed below that amount they would sell enough cars to make a profit. Thus, except for the bulge on the front hood everything was derived from the Spitfire. Michelotti simply carried the lines back from the top of the windshield to the rear bumper.

When it came time to select a motor Triumph again reached into the parts bin. They pulled out

---

GT6 MK 1

ENGINE
Type: 6-cylinder, in line, cast iron cylinder block and head, four main bearings
Bore x Stroke: mm/inches: 74.7x76/2.94x2.99
Displacement: cc/cubic inches: 1998/122
Valve Operation: ohv, pushrod operation
Compression Ratio: 9.5:1
Carburetion: 2 Zenith-Strombergs
BHP (mfr): 95 at 5000rpm

CHASSIS & DRIVETRAIN
Transmission: 4-speed with optional overdrive, synchro on all forward gears
Axle Ratio: 3.89:1, 3.27 optional
Rear Suspension: independent swing axles, transverse leaf spring, radius rods, telescopic shocks
Front Suspension: independent coil springs, wishbones, telescopic shocks, sway bar

GENERAL
Wheelbase: 83"
Overall Length: 145"
Track: Front: 49"
       Rear: 48"
Brakes: Front: 9.7" discs
        Rear: 8"x1.25" drums
Wheel Size: 4.5x13 pressed steel wheels, wire wheels optional
Tire Size: 155-13 radial ply
Weight: 1,970 lbs.

PERFORMANCE
Acceleration: 0-30: 4.4 seconds, 0-60: 12.3 seconds
Top Speed: 107mph with overdrive

This very early GT6 had both the wire wheels and the whitewall tires. Notice that the earliest cars lacked side marker lights. The bulge in the center accommodated the six-cylinder engine. Also, the grille was composed of horizontal slats to distinguish it from the Spitfire but the basic layout of all the mechanicals was very similar to the Spitfire. These early cars were the cleanest and simplest design. *Plain English Archive.*

the motor from the Vitesse (Sports Six in the United States). This engine started life as a 1596cc unit, but the 1.6-liter engine was never really considered. Instead, an expanded 2-liter unit was used to give the car a true GT feel.

Likewise, Triumph also changed the Spitfire's suspension to get away from the wagon wheel ride of the early Spitfires. This wasn't going to be a Spitfire with a six-cylinder engine, but rather a true GT car for under $3,000. The only problem was that nobody had figured out who they were going to sell the car to.

The engine turned out to be the best part of the GT. They achieved 95hp with 117 feet-pounds of torque. Nothing great by today's standards but you have to remember Porsche was only getting 160hp out of the 2-liter 911S engine, a racing motor, that could just barely be used on the street. With the Triumph you get a nice smooth running engine with very little vibration, minimal shifting, and a relaxed highway cruising speed.

This picture not only shows the hood bulge, but also the louvers. There was a hope that this would keep the underhood temperature within reason. *Author collection.*

Very few GT6s had the Triumph magnesium wheels installed. Considering what they did for the appearance of the car, perhaps Triumph should have made them standard equipment. These wheels are still around at some flea markets but don't expect them to be cheap. Don't be fooled by the knock-off caps; right behind them are the bolts that actually hold the wheels on. *Plain English Archive.*

GT6 MK 2/GT6+

ENGINE
Type: 6-cylinder, in line, cast iron cylinder block and head, four main bearings
Bore x Stroke: mm/inches: 74.7x76/2.94x2.99
Displacement: cc/cubic inches: 1998/122
Valve Operation: ohv, pushrod operation
Compression Ratio: 9.25:1
Carburetion: 2 Zenith-Strombergs
BHP (mfr): 104 at 5300rpm, 95 at 4700rpm for federalized version

CHASSIS & DRIVETRAIN
Transmission: 4-speed with optional overdrive, synchro on all forward gears
Axle Ratio: 3.89:1 with overdrive, 3.27:1 without overdrive
Rear Suspension: independent rear suspension by transverse leaf and lower wishbones
Front Suspension: independent coil springs, wishbones, telescopic shocks, sway bar

GENERAL
Wheelbase: 83"
Overall Length: 145"
Track: Front: 49"
         Rear: 49"
Brakes: Front: 9.7" discs
          Rear: 8"x1.25" drums
Wheel Size: 4.5x13 pressed steel wheels, wire wheels optional
Tire Size: 155-13 radial ply
Weight: 1,907 lbs.

PERFORMANCE
Acceleration: 0-30: 4.0 seconds, 0-60: 11.0 seconds
Top Speed: 109mph with overdrive

This is a nicely restored engine in an early GT. GT carburetors were twin Zenith-Strombergs. The displacement was 1998cc and the power 95hp at 5000rpm. Placing a six-cylinder engine in this chassis wasn't as easy as it first looked. The radiator had to be pushed to the very front, and the inlet pipe to the block curved sharply to the radiator. The radiator cap was located on a tank separate from the radiator. *Author collection.*

The only problem is that to utilize all this performance you'll need to locate some quality premium gas since the compression ratio is 9.5:1. Octane boosters are really not the answer and racing gas is really just too hard to locate. Today's modern gasolines are really marginal with this engine.

One useful feature of the GT6 is that the rear hatch allows you to load and remove luggage with very little effort. The same goes for access to the engine which retains the Spitfire type hood.

The major drawback with the GT6 was that the basic design created a space problem. If you're much over five foot nine inches the car is just too tight a fit. If you're taller than five foot eleven inches then you want a different car. Six footers need not even bother applying.

Basically the GT6 is a really marvelous little car built for small people. One writer put it rather nicely when he pointed out that "...Triumph continually revised the seating arrangements but there was no way that the GT6 would ever stop being a car built for small people."

Now the wheels get really plain. A basic fact of life is that for people with limited time and money these are the best wheels to have on any car. They're easy to maintain and if you should ever bend one it will be easy to replace. *Plain English Archive.*

The other problem was ventilation. Even with the vent windows and the flow-through ventilation system, cockpit heat was a problem when it was 80 degrees or more outside. This was a car designed for the British climate. Riding in a GT6 in August you understand that the British certainly never visited Texas.

A major improvement, and a better buy for collectors, is the Mk 2 of 1969-70. Outside of the US this was know as the GT6+. Despite the fact it looks a lot like the first car, Triumph made a lot of improvements with the GT6. The GT6 was a classic case of "Engineering by Triumph—Development by Customers."

An improved ventilation system was added to the GT6+, and the seats now reclined. Wire wheels and the overdrive transmission remained as options. The earlier polished-walnut dash gave way to a dull finish. On the US models the bumper was raised, similar to the Mk 3 Spitfire. With a lot of effort some people have moved this bumper back to its original height, something that hardly seems worth all the trouble.

Under all the sheet metal the GT6+ kept the existing chassis and the transverse leaf spring. The big difference was that the driveshafts were no longer fixed in length. A big rubber doughnut was mounted part way down the shaft in an effort to control torque and road shock. A complicated but well-located lower wishbone pivoted between the chassis and the hubs. The feel of the GT on the road took a giant leap forward and even began to remind some people of the mini E-Type concept, especially people with vivid imaginations.

While 16,000 Mk 1s were produced the GT6+/Mk 2 saw only 12,000 units. The time had

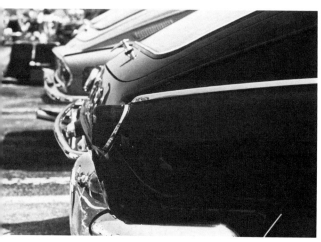

The taillights were the same as on the early TR, as well as on the Spitfire. In the background is a Mk 3. *Author collection.*

come for a new Mk 3 version, complete with the Kamm back end that Triumph had grown so fond of.

This Mk 3 model used all the body changes from the Mk IV Spitfire which gave the rear wheel arches a slight flare and the flat-black grille. The taillights were also changed as a result of this new body shell.

GT6 MK 3

ENGINE
Type: 6-cylinder, in line, cast iron cylinder block and head, four main bearings
Bore x Stroke: mm/inches: 74.7x76/2.94x2.99
Displacement: cc/cubic inches: 1998/122
Valve Operation: ohv, pushrod operation
Compression Ratio: 9.25:1
Carburetion: 2 Zenith-Strombergs
BHP (mfr): 104 at 5300rpm, 90 at 4700rpm for federalized version

CHASSIS & DRIVETRAIN
Transmission: 4-speed with optional overdrive, synchro on all forward gears
Axle Ratio: 3.27:1 without overdrive, 3.89 with overdrive
Rear Suspension: independent rear suspension by transverse leaf and lower wishbones
Front Suspension: independent coil springs, wishbones, telescopic shocks, sway bar

GENERAL
Wheelbase: 83"
Overall Length: 149"
Track: Front: 49"
      Rear: 49"

One other minor change was that in 1973 the overdrive switch was moved to the gearshift lever. Power brakes also came along in 1973. No great changes, just small improvements.

Outside of the United States the horsepower remained at 104hp for the entire life of the GT. The US wasn't so lucky. In 1971 it went down to 90hp and in 1972 it was further reduced to 79hp. In one last attempt to cut production costs, the rear suspension was changed to the pivoting spring similar to the Spitfire 1500.

All of these changes to the final version mean that the Mk 2 version is the best car to own. With the Mk 2 you get all the improvements, without the cost-saving measures. This was the best of all the GT6s and it still is today.

The major problem with today's GTs is rust. Just as most of the Spitfires rusted away the same problems afflicted the GT6. Especially check the area under the spare tire. Another area is behind the rear seats where the suspension bolts to the body. We're talking about serious rust areas here.

The good part is that these suspension mount towers can be purchased separately. There's no need to throw the whole car away, just plan on spending a lot of time and money.

The body shell is more complex than the Spitfire. This in turn means more rust problems. Also, closed cars never seem to truly dry out the way the open Spitfires do. Check every area where you think water might be hiding before you write any checks.

Another problem is that by now most of the axle doughnuts have deteriorated, and in some cases are cracked all the way through. If you have any doubts about their condition replace them at the earliest opportunity. If one of these doughnuts finally does break loose, it can create a lot of unexpected excitement.

The engine is a delight and shouldn't give any problems. If the car's been cared for about the only potential problem is a blown head gasket. It's not at all unusual for the gasket to break between the 5th and 6th cylinder. In severe cases this can mean a cracked cylinder head.

If you hear transmission noise first check the transmission tunnel. A loose, or broken, tunnel cover is far more common than an actual broken transmission. Generally the transmission and differential are fairly robust. Keep in mind though that repairs can get real expensive real fast. Couple this with the fact that the value of the car won't increase very quickly while you own it. Major repairs mean that you'll take a substantial loss when you sell the car.

The GT is one of those cars that receives little attention from the collector. Triumph still means

TR. When the car was new it was generally avoided by customers who were willing to spend the extra money on a TR6, or they just didn't fit the GT. Either way they missed out on a nice car. This is still the case. Triumph collectors focus on the TR series cars and neglect cars like the Spitfire, the Stag, and the GT6. This Triumph GT is really a car for the individual who likes a small touring car, not the serious collector looking for financial gain.

The biggest problem with the car will be the price of parts. While you can buy the car for a reasonable price, the price of these parts will be roughly the same as those of a TR6. This means that it's very easy to spend more on restoring a GT than the car is worth. You should make sure you really like the car before you start pumping money into it.

This also means that you should buy the best example you can locate. A basket case GT will not only kill your bank balance but make your Triumph experience an unpleasant one. Buy a GT6 because you like it, not because of its intrinsic monetary value.

In England it was called the Mk 2 and in the United States it was called the GT6+. Not all of them used the silly wheelcovers. The side lights were there because the United States government said they had to be. *Plain English Archive.*

The Mk 2 got the fake Rostyle wheelcovers, which were a low point in Triumph design, as well as a new set of louvers on the side. The bumper was raised to the style of the Spitfire Mk 3. *Author collection.*

The front of the GT6 Mk 3 got the smoothed fenders of the Spitfire Mk IV, not to mention the rubber bumpers. Next to the car is a Mk 1 GT. *Author collection.*

The car is just as easy to load things into as it is for work
to be done on the engine. *Plain English Archive*.

The fender slots were removed on the Mk 3 and a BL badge added. The wheels got the TR6 look and the Michelotti family look was applied to the rear end. *Plain English Archive.*

The rear end was changed on the GT Mk 3 and the Spitfire Mk IV. The opportunity was used to blend the roof into the tail a little differently, and to add extractor vents behind the window. The fuel filler neck was relocated to the rear fender. *Author collection.*

Chapter 20

Stag

Ten years ago these cars virtually disappeared. No one wanted a Stag. Today you'll find a number of restored Stags on the market, and there will be even more over the next decade. This is one of the most unique and nicest Triumphs around. There's also more interest in the Stag than in the last twenty years.

The only problem with the Stag, and it was a major one, was that the Stag was the wrong car, at the wrong time. The Stag was an anomaly, neither a sports car nor a sedan. It wasn't a high speed coupe, nor was it a convertible. It was a nice car but there was never a reason to buy one of these cars.

The Stag sold much better in England, which is still the case today. The biggest problem with owning a Stag in the United States is finding someone to help you work on the car. This is no small

The Stag interior was the finest ever used in a modern Triumph. The gauges may look familiar to a TR6 owner.

The whole interior was quality leather and nicely designed. *Author collection.*

This is a factory photo for the German market. The cheap hubcaps were installed on all the cars outside of the American market. Also, the Stag emblem on the rear fender is used to cover the hole for the American side marker. This is the version with the hardtop installed. Think of it as Triumph's effort at a low cost GT car. *Plain English Archive.*

problem. Since so few cars were sold in America the level of Stag expertise is very limited.

The Stag was the idea of Giovanni Michelotti who wanted to produce a sporting version of the Triumph 200 Saloon. He enlisted Chief Engineer Harry Webster in the cause and together they pushed the idea to the Triumph directors. The result of all this political effort was a plan that called for selling 12,000 Stags a year. The reality was that they sold 25,877 cars—in seven years. They only missed their marketing projection by over 70,000 units. Even worse was the fact that only 6,780 Stags were ever delivered to the American dealers.

Part of the problem was the turmoil in the British auto industry. When Leyland merged with Rover the new company found itself with two V-8 engines. Triumph was allowed to keep the 3-liter engine for the Stag while everyone else got the old

3.5-liter Buick engine. In retrospect this was the wrong decision. If the Stag had received the Rover engine Triumph might have avoided some major problems.

Engine problems were the biggest affliction, especially in the United States. Overheating was the major problem, probably attributable in part to the fact the English never really understood the American climate. The other reason was the way the cylinder head was designed. Any overheating problem would lead to a warped cylinder head. Then, adding insult to injury, you couldn't find anyone who could repair the car. In which case you had a car that was worthless.

There are two thing you need to know if you own a Stag. First, torquing the cylinder head bolts is a part of routine maintenance. This needs to be done often. Secondly, the minute the car overheats pull off the road.

STAG

ENGINE
Type: 90-degree V-8
Bore x Stroke: mm/inches: 86x65/3.38x2.54
Displacement: cc/cubic inches: 2997/182.9
Valve Operation: ohv, single overhead cam per bank
Compression Ratio: 8.8:1
Carburetion: dual Stromberg IV
BHP (mfr): 145 at 5500rpm

CHASSIS & DRIVETRAIN
Transmission: 4-speed with optional overdrive, Borg Warner automatic optional
Rear Suspension: independent, semitrailing arms, coil springs, telescopic shock absorbers
Axle Ratio: 3.70:1
Front Suspension: independent, MacPherson struts, coil springs, telescopic shocks

GENERAL
Wheelbase: 100"
Overall Length: 174"
Track: Front: 52.5"
      Rear: 52.9"
Brakes: Front: 10.6" discs
      Rear: 9.0"x 2.25 " drums
Wheel Size: 5.5"x14"
Tire Size: 185 HR 14
Weight: 2,800 lbs.

PERFORMANCE
Acceleration: 0-30: 3.5 seconds, 0-60: 9.6 seconds
Top Speed: 122mph

This is the American Stag. The side marker lights were installed in the fenders and a Stag badge was placed below the light. In Europe, the badge covered the hole in the fender. *Author collection.*

If you stop driving at the first sign of overheating you can probably save the engine. If you fail to notice the problem, or ignore the problem you'll destroy the motor. The cylinder heads will warp and you be facing a major repair bill.

Also, the timing chains for the Stag needed replacing about every 25,000 miles, something the average buyer wasn't prepared for. The fact that one-half of the Stags imported into the United States had major engine work performed under warranty did very little for the reputation of the car. There's very little chance today that you'll find a Stag that hasn't had major engine work performed. The quality of that work will vary from car to car. The Stag motor is still a potential problem twenty years later.

If you're thinking about buying a Stag let the engine idle for at least fifteen minutes. If the gauge goes into the high zone, walk away from the car. Trust me, you don't want a Stag with an overheating problem.

Bad timing chains are harder to detect. These chains made a lot of noise when the were brand new. Best to err on the side of caution. If the owner can't produce a set of receipts for a new timing chain then plan on spending some money in the very near future.

The Stag had virtually disappeared when I wrote the first edition of this book. During the early nineties they started to make a strong comeback. Today you can expect to see several nice Stags at almost any Triumph gathering. Interest is increasing in these cars every year.

You have to accept the Triumph Stag for what it is, not what you want it to be. This is no sports car. The Stag is really not even a high speed touring car. The Stag is simply a nice looking moderately fast, moderately comfortable highway car. Owning a nice example can be a lot of fun. Owning a bad example will make you swear off British cars forever.

The hardtop has been removed and the padded roll bar is displayed. An accent strip was added along the side and the alloy wheels installed. In this picture both the BL badge and the stainless rocker panel are in place. *Plain English Archive.*

An alternative to the hardtop was the convertible. The top folded down into the trunk behind the rear seats, which had a hard lid to cover the top. Few cars offered the alternatives of putting two different roofs over your head. *Author collection.*

Here's a Stag that has three windows on the soft top.
Author collection.

Triumph finally gave up on the steel wheels with hubcaps. They decided to replace the cheap wheel with this alloy version. *Author collection.*

Chapter 21

★★★★★	Factory cars
★★★★	Private cars

Factory Racers and Former Prototypes

This is the one area where Triumphs have really gained in value since the first edition of this book. Vintage racing was just getting started in the mid-eighties. Old race cars were simply cars that you couldn't drive on the street. Their racing days were long gone and there was only minimal interest in the old Triumph race cars. No one really wanted them.

Today the most expensive Triumphs you can own are the vintage racers. Vintage racing is soaring

Triumph used racing to promote the sports car line. Here at the 1959 Le Mans race is the TR3S. The car looked very similar to a TR3A at a distance but it used a longer wheelbase and fiberglass body. *Plain English Archive.*

When Triumph returned to Le Mans in 1960 it had a new body on the cars. The mechanicals were very similar to the previous year except for a wider track. *Plain English Archive.*

in popularity. Close to five hundred race cars show up at the major events, and the crowds are the largest in racing. Vintage car races generally draw larger crowds than the Indy cars. All this means that vintage Triumphs will continue to gain in value.

We start with the factory race cars. These cars have a significant history and they bring the highest prices. Triumph always had a strong racing effort. Triumph used motorsports to create an image. They never missed an opportunity to demonstrate their products at race tracks around the world.

If you're in the market for one of the old factory race cars make sure that it comes with a lot of paper work. You should be able to trace a continuous history of the car from the time it left the factory racing effort. This should include letters from the people who raced them, and the mechanics who built them.

You're paying top dollar for one of these cars. A questionable history will bring the value down

to what you might pay for a nice TR4. Fraud is a fact of life with vintage race cars. It's not all that difficult to "create" a factory racer. The only difference between reality and fantasy is the paperwork. Be sure that you get what you pay for, because you're going to being paying a lot for a former factory race car.

Restoring one of the factory racers is a very time-consuming project. Don't even think about doing one of these cars as your first Triumph project. Just collecting all the relevant information will take you longer than the average TR3 restoration.

A big question is what constitutes original condition? Restoring a race car is similar to restoring an axe that's had three handles and two heads. Race cars changed from season to season, not to mention race to race.

You simply have to pick a race and restore the car to that configuration. You'll also find that many of the parts on this race car were originally made

Known as the Macau car, this Spitfire was assembled in 1965. The factory was persuaded to build the car from leftover spare parts from the Le Mans effort. Before the car left England it was clocked at the Motor Industry Proving Grounds at over 130mph. Rumor has it that the car is currently in California. *Plain English Archive.*

from scratch. This means that you'll end up with a lot of hand fabrication work. You'll also find yourself removing parts that previous owners installed.

These factory racers were usually sold to private individuals after a season of racing. The cars then passed down through a succession of owners, all making their own little modifications. Your task is to restore the car to its original factory configuration. This will be no small undertaking.

The basic fact is that restoring a factory race or rally car is the most complex, and detailed, Triumph restoration you can possibly undertake. It will take more time and resources than most people are willing to commit to a hobby.

After the Triumph factory racers you'll find the American Group 44 race cars bringing high prices. This was the American factory effort. These were usually the fastest Triumphs in the world. If the Triumph was really an American car manufactured in England it's only fitting that the Americans built the fastest Triumph race cars.

Group 44 had long racing association with Triumph. They started racing TR3s and campaigned TR8s even after Triumph ceased production. For twenty years they had sponsorship from Quaker State oil and raced the products of Triumph/Leyland/JRT/Jaguar. The companies would change names but Group 44 was always there racing the current models. They raced every Triumph TR sports car, and all the different variations of the Spitfire. This was a big league racing effort.

There are a lot of Group 44 cars floating around the world at this point. There are also some replica cars out there so be very careful. If you're thinking about purchasing one of these old race cars make certain that it was originally built by Group 44. Fortunately, Bob Tullius is still in business and can be easily contacted. If he can't verify the car as being authentic then walk away from the purchase.

Next in the pecking order are the club racers. These are the SCCA sports cars raced in America, as well as the local clubs in England. These are Triumphs that have an authentic racing history but never achieved fame and fortune. These are also the cars that have been passed down from one racer to the next. They've usually been modified a great deal over the years and will require a major effort to put back into decent shape.

These club racers should come with a documented history. If there's no written history the price should reflect that fact. It does very little good to simply say that "the car was raced by some guy in the Midwest during the early seventies." That really isn't a history. It's just rumor.

The reason a documented history is important is that in the future more vintage racing associations are going to require proof of an authentic history. Vintage sports car racing is getting so popular that many tracks are already having more cars show up than they can reasonably accommodate.

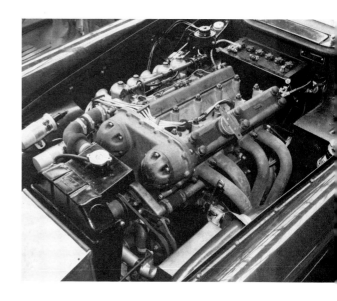

This Triumph was styled by Michelotti, with the Italian firm Conrero building the tube-frame chassis. The engine is the same as found in the LeMans cars. There are rumors that the factory tested this car at 142mph. This car has changed very little since 1961. It spent most of its life in America but is currently owned by John Ames in England. *Plain English Archive.*

One constant over the years for Triumph was Bob Tullius. Here he is on the grid in 1962 at Marlboro in a TR4.

This is one of the few pictures of a Group 44 car not painted white. *Plain English Archive.*

Here at Riverside in 1966 the team was racing a TR4A (number 103). Even though the TR4As were not any faster than the TR4s, Group 44 always made an effort to

race the latest car being sold. The fact that they had a good relationship with Standard-Triumph didn't hurt at all. *Plain English Archive.*

Brian Fuerstenau next to the Group 44 Spitfire Mk 3 at
Lime Rock. *Plain English Archive.*

The largest moving Quaker State billboard in the world. If it was a Triumph, Group 44 raced it, as well as hauled it in the Quaker State transporter. Here are a Spitfire, a GT6, and a TR6. There is also an unidentifiable car with a funny octagonal badge in the lineup. *Group 44 photo.*

This was the factory effort at Sebring in 1963. They used the Surrey Top for racing. This style of metal top is one of the most difficult items to locate today. Triumph entered three TR4s and each one had about 145hp, as compared to 105hp in stock form. They could go from 0 to 60mph in under nine seconds. One reason for this acceleration was the 4.55:1 rear axle ratio, but it limited the cars to a top speed of 108mph. *Plain English Archive.*

One easy way to control the number of entries is to simply state that only cars with genuine racing histories are allowed to race. Usually all the current competitors are allowed to continue racing. New people now have to document that they have a real race car.

There's still one more category of car we haven't talked about—the rally cars. Triumph always maintained a strong rally effort in Europe. These old rally cars are valuable. The proviso is that they're more valuable in Europe than in the United States. Europe has a strong rally tradition, something that never happened in the United States.

There's a major effort in Europe that centers around historic rallying. Authentic factory rally cars are a major part of that effort. In the United States no such effort exists. You could probably run a rally car at some vintage racing events, but with little success.

This means that all the old rally cars will be most valuable in Europe. In fact there are very few, if any, in the United States. This points up the fact that value is attached to what you can do with the car.

This single fact is what has pushed the value of old race cars to new levels. When you can do something fun with an old Triumph race car the value increases. Vintage racing is one of the fastest growing areas in the entire car hobby so you can look for even more appreciation in the value of racing Triumphs.

Author collection.

Ken Slagle ran semi-factory effort with this Spitfire. He won an SCCA national championship with this car, and then went on to a total factory effort with a TR7. A club racer with a winning history can be a valuable car to own. The trick is returning the car to the original configuration. *Plain English Archive.*

Here's a TR250 effort. Notice that not only are all the modern day decals missing from this car, but there isn't a single transporter in sight. This is a good example of the most valuable TR250 you could own. This car is out there someplace. If it ever goes up for sale prepare to spend more than you ever thought reasonable to spend on a Triumph. *Plain English Archive.*

This TR4, shown at Vineland, New Jersey, in 1965, and driven by Dick Stockton, is currently resting in a garage in central Pennsylvania. Stockton was a constant factor in club racing during the sixties. While he was never a factory driver he always had a good relationship with the Triumph racing program. This car is an excellent candidate for a vintage racing program. *Plain English Archive.*

This is an example of a club racer that lacks an outstanding history. Cars such as this can be very nice. The lack of prominence means that the car should be a lot cheaper than the former winners. Try to find a race car in as complete condition as possible. If you have to replace any of the racing parts your budget goes to another level. *Author collection.*

Vintage racing is about having fun. No one is going to get upset because these wheels were made about three decades after the car. Most vintage racing groups will not let the cars run slick tires. These are the latest high-tech tires from B.F. Goodrich. The irony is that these tires may actually stick to the pavement far better than the slicks of the mid-seventies. *Author collection.*

This was the Triumph factory effort for the Shell 4000 Rally, which began in Vancouver and ended in Montreal. Once again notice that the factory was using the Surrey Top. The vents in the fender were a standard factory rally car modification. These allowed the hot engine compartment air to exit to the outside. Notice that the car is also equipped with the factory magnesium racing wheels. *Plain English Archive.*

"Kas" Kastner, formerly competitions manager for Standard-Triumph in the United States, making a final adjustment on the Shell 4000 Rally car. The fender vent is visible from this angle. Also obvious is the Clayton chassis dynamometer in the background. *Plain English Archive.*

The Triumph TR-4
Out of 6 Sports Car Club of America Class D Divisions, the TR-4 won three—Midwest, Northeast, Pacific Coast. (Bob Tullius, in #44, became Northeast Champion for the 4th straight year.)

The hot new TR-4A was the Class D Modified Champion in the only division entered—Pacific Coast.

The Triumph Spitfire
She's the Class G Champion in three Divisions—Midwest, Southwest, Southeast. And she placed second in two others.

The Triumph TR-3
"Old Reliable" is the Class F Champion in four Divisions—Midwest, Northeast, Pacific Coast, Southwest.

Triumph triumphs again in 1965

(See your local Triumph dealer for a test-drive of any one of our 4 great models.)

Flash from Daytona...1965 American Road Race of Champions... Triumph sweeps Class D Production. Wins D Modified and F Production.

1965 was a big year for Triumph. This ad was used in all the major auto magazines in February of 1966. Racing was about selling cars, and for Triumph this worked. In an era of high-tech Japanese cars we forget that average people could afford to race Triumphs. *Author collection.*

Here the factory team is making last-minute adjustments before the 1958 Alpine Rally. Authentic factory rally cars are difficult to locate, let alone purchase. They also command a high price, which means you need to be very careful before you let go of your money. *Plain English Archive.*

A row of rally cars outside the Triumph factory. Apparently they haven't been registered. The extra lights were factory installed only on the competition cars. *Plain English Archive.*

In 1959 a rally was run from New York to Reno. Here Alex Thompson and Bob Halmi are preparing for the event. Door handles became standard on the TR3A. The front parking lights were rounded, and the headlight rims were widened. They also used the ever-popular Michelin X radial tires. *Plain English Archive.*

Ken Richardson looking over preparations for the 1959 Monte Carlo Rally. *Plain English Archive.*

Sebring called for a more serious factory effort. This was the Spitfire GT Coupe that was used at the Florida race in 1964. Finding one of these cars today would be a major coup . Consider this type of Triumph one of the best possible purchases. *Plain English Archive.*

TRIUMPH GT-6 DP

TRIUMPH SPITFIRE FP, GP

MG MIDGET FP, GP

TRIUMPH TR-6 CP

AUSTIN HEALEY SPRITE HP, GP, FP

AUSTIN MINI CS, DS

MGB EP

BRITISH LEYLAND RACING MODELS

By 1971, Standard-Triumph had become a part of the British Leyland conglomerate. Any one of the cars in this picture would make a wonderful vintage racing effort. Notice the lack of huge fender flares and air dams. The cars actually looked like the Triumph you drove on the street. This is what makes vintage racing so popular. It's really not about racing, it's about going back to another era—an era when the budgets were under a million dollars, and people had fun doing it. *Plain English Archive.*

A pleasant way to spend your weekend is driving your TR3 around one of America's race tracks. Remember,

Triumphs are sports cars, not trophies. They should be driven, not stored in garages. *Author collection.*

162

Triumph Clubs

Six-Pac
303 Longfellow Drive
Lancaster, PA 17602
USA

Stag Club of America
P.O. Box 26453
Tucson, AZ 85726
USA

Stag Owners Club
53 Cyprus Road
Faversham, Kent
ME13 8HD
England
    This is strictly for Stag owners They publish the usual newsletter and offer an insurance plan for the English members. They currently have over 6,000 members.

TR8 Car Club of America
266 Linden Street
Rochester, NY 14620
USA
    They publish a quarterly newsletter which includes technical data. Since you may be the only TR8 owner within a one hundred mile radius you should seriously think about joining this club. Where else are you going to find out how to take care of your TR8?

Vintage Triumph Register
15218 Warren Avenue
Dearborn, MI 48126
USA
    This club welcomes all Triumphs. There are local chapters all around the United States that operate under the VTR umbrella.

Club Triumph
86 Waggon Road
Hadley Wood, Herts
EN4 OPP
England
    This club welcomes all Triumph owners. They publish a newsletter and offer an insurance program. This is the largest British Triumph club, with numerous regional chapters.

Triumph Mayflower Review
19 Broadway North,
Walsall, West Midlands WS1 2QG
England
    This club is over twenty years old with members in all areas of the world. There's a newsletter called *Flower Power*, which is published periodically. If you're an American with a Mayflower this is a club you need to consider.

Triumph Roadster Club
The Woodlands
Taddington, Nr Buxton
Derbyshire SK17 9UD
England
    This is the oldest Triumph club in Britain. They're dedicated to the preservation of the 1946-49 Roadsters. They've managed to locate over a quarter of these early cars produced by Triumph. They also publish a monthly newsletter called the *Roadster Review*.

Triumph Register of America
1641 N. Memorial Drive
Lancaster, OH 43130
USA
    This is strictly for the TR2 and TR3 owners. It's the only American organization dedicated to

the early Triumph sports cars.

TR Drivers' Club
39 Brook Street
Benson, Oxfordshire OX9 6LQ
England
    This club has been in existence for over fifteen years. This is a large club that specializes in the TR models.

Triumph Razoredge Owners Club
62 Seaward Avenue
Barton on Sea
Hampshire
England
    This club publishes a newsletter called *The Globe*. While the club is centered in England they welcome American owners. Since there are so very few of these cars in the United States anyone with a Razoredge must consider joining.

TR Register
1B Hawksworth
Southmead Industrial Park
Didcot, Oxon Ox11 7HR
England

This club welcomes all TR owners from 2 through 8. They also publish a quarterly newsletter, called "TR Action." There are more than 7,000 members, and the club has a full-time professional manager.

Triumph Sporting Owners Club
57 Rothiemey Road
Flixton, Urmston
Manchester, Greater Manchester
M31 3JY
England

Triumph Sports Six Club
Main Street
Lubenham, Leicestershire
LE16 9TF
England
    This is the club for Triumph Heralds, Vitesses, Spitfires, and GT6s. The club was formed in 1977 and has over 18,000 members. A third of the members drive Spitfires. The club publishes a newsletter called the *Courier*.

Recommended Triumph Books and Periodicals

Books

Brooklands Triumph Cars
    By R.M. Clarke, Brooklands Books, Surrey, England.
Triumph GT6 1966-74
Triumph Stag 1970-80
Triumph TR2 & TR3 1952-60
Triumph TR4, TR5, TR250 1961-68
Triumph TR7 & TR8 1975-82
Triumph Vitesse 1962-71
    This is a well-produced series of road tests and articles compiled from a variety of car magazines from around the world. The only problem with the series is that there are no articles from *Motor Trend* or, more importantly, *Sports Car Graphic*. Clarke copies the original articles and puts a decade's worth in a book. It sure saves you a lot of time attempting to find all these articles on your own.

Triumph Gold Portfolios
    Edited by R. M. Clarke.
Triumph Spitfire 1962-80
Triumph TR6 1969-76
    This is essentially a new package for the Brooklands Series. Each book consists of reprinted articles from the different time periods.

The Triumph Spitfire
    By Michael Cook, TAB Books, Blue Ridge Summit, PA.
    This is the best book written on the American Spitfires. Cook was the American public relations director for Triumph and Leyland. Cook knows Triumphs better than anyone in the United States. The only problem is that the book has been out of print for some time. The Roadster Factory printed a special edition of this book and may still have a few copies remaining.

TR for Triumph
    By Chris Harvey, Haynes Publishing Group, England.
    What a wonderful book. The best part is the lavish use of color. It covers the full TR range and deals with the problems you might encounter, racing preparation, and restoration. It's a very complete book and should be on your shelf.

Triumph Cars: The Complete 75-Year History
    By Richard Langworth and Graham Robson, Motor Racing Publication, Ltd., London, England.
    This is the only complete history of the marque. There are a lot of interviews with Triumph engineers and designers, the only people able to tell you the story from inside the company. This book is currently out of print and you'll have to look for it in the flea markets.

Triumph Stag
    By Andrew Morland
    There are even fewer books about Stags than there were cars produced. If you want the complete Stag bookshelf it will include about three books. You might as well have all of them.

Original Triumph TR
    By Bill Piggott, Bay View Books Ltd., 13a Bridgeland Street, Devon, England
    This is the single best book available on the TR series. A tremendous amount of effort went into researching the TR series. If you're restoring any of the TR series cars then you'll need this book. This is the sort of book that concours judges use to resolve controversies. It's the sort of book I use because all the color pictures are so well done. If you don't have this book on your shelf then your Triumph library is incomplete.

Practical Classics Series
Spitfire
Triumph Herald 1959-1971
Triumph Herald/Vitesse
Triumph Stag

This has been a nice series. The practical advice is well worth the price of the book. While it often seems a little short on information it should be on your shelf before you start doing any serious work on your Triumph.

Road & Track on Triumph Sports Cars.
Triumph Sports Cars 1953-67
Triumph Sports Cars 1967-74
Triumph Sports Cars 1974-82

The Brooklands Series has been so successful over the years that *Road & Track* now offers its own reprint series. The reproduction quality is better than the Brooklands Series. The only problem is that *Road & Track* never met a car that they didn't like. Even when a car is an abomination they feel the need for lavish praise.

The Triumph TRs: A Collector's Guide

By Graham Robson, Motor Racing Publication, Ltd., London, England.

A careful look at the TR series by a man who worked for the company and once served in its competitions department. This is a good solid examination of the TRs from the TR2 to the TR7. Robson's book is one of the few books you *must* read before you buy a TR.

Triumph Spitfire and GT6

By Graham Robson, Osprey Publishing, London, England.

This is a counterpart to Robson's Collector's Guide except it deals with the Spitfire. There are chapters by Richard Langworth on the American history of Triumph. Once again Robson has written an essential book for the Spitfire/GT6 fans.

Triumph Stag Super Profile

By James Taylor, Haynes Publishing Group, Somerset, England.

This is a nice basic book on the Stag. It even has a picture of a racing Stag, the rarest Stag of all. You would be foolish to buy a Stag without looking at this book. This book is not only inexpensive, but it contains a wealth of information about the Stag.

Periodicals
Automobile
120 E. Liberty Street
Ann Arbor, MI 48104
(313) 994-3500

The focus here is on upscale modern cars. Don't expect to find too much about old cars in this magazine.

Autoweek
1400 Woodbridge
Detroit, MI 48207-3187
(313) 446-6000

Autoweek is a weekly news magazine. It covers all the latest news and very little about old cars. The back page of each issue, "Escape Road," does deal with a different vintage car each week. These are usually significant examples of automobile history. An excellent news magazine, but very little on old English cars.

British Car
P.O. Box 9099
Canoga Park, CA 91309

This is the only American magazine that focuses on English cars. It's a bi-monthly magazine that you need to subscribe to if you're working with old English cars.

Car and Driver
2002 Hogback Road
Ann Arbor, MI 48104
(313) 944-0055

A monthly news magazine. They do a good job of covering the modern car scene, but seldom, if ever, have articles about old English cars.

Classic and Sportscar
Haymarket Publishing Ltd.
3-4 Hardwick Street
London, EC1R 4RY
England

This is one of the best magazines on the market for old English sports cars. They may not always have an article about your particular car, but you'll still want to read it every month in an effort to keep well informed on the subject of English classic cars.

Grassroots Motorsports
P.O. Box 5907
Daytona Beach, FL 32118
(904) 673-4148

A small magazine that is the personal vision of the editor. The good part is that they like old English cars. The emphasis is on inexpensive racing.

Don't look for much dealing with restoration, but if you want to make your car perform better take a look at it.

Hemmings Motor News
Box 100
Bennington, VT 05201

The is *the* book for the old car hobby. Hundreds of pages of classified ads every month. There are people who claim they read every page—every month. It's hard to find on most newsstands so you may have to get a subscription. If you're buying an old car you *must* read Hemmings.

Practical Classics
Bushfield House
Orton Centre
Peterborough, PE2 5UW
England

This is a very basic do-it-yourself magazine for people who are restoring their own cars. The emphasis is on the practical. A very worthwhile magazine dealing with affordable cars.

Road & Track
1499 Monrovia
Newport Beach, CA 92663

This is the oldest car magazine in the United States. They print very little about old English cars. Reading *Road & Track* is a little like reading *The New York Times*, it's boring but all the recent news about cars around the world is in the magazine.

Thoroughbred & Classic Cars
Kings Reach Tower
Stamford Street
London, SE1 9LS
England

This monthly magazine has been around for a long time. It deals with the history of the cars. They do very little with do-it-yourself articles, but rather focus on the historical development of the cars, and the personalities of the people in the industry.

Parts and Service Sources

Apple Hydraulics
1610 Middle Road
Calveton, NY 11933
(800) 369-9515

These are the shock experts. They're just about the only people in the United States who rebuild old lever shocks. They will also rebuild the shock links. After your last Fall drive remove the shocks and send them to Apple Hydraulics for a Winter rebuild.

British Auto Interiors
1555 Elm Street
Manchester, NH 03101
(603) 622-1050

Peter Gould and his staff have a nice array of TR interior pieces. They also have a line of upholstery for the Spitfires.

British Parts Northwest
4105 S.E. Lafayette Highway
Dayton, OR 97114
(503) 864-2001

This company carries a full range of parts for British cars. The only catalog they publish is for Triumph cars. That tells you where their loyalty lies.

Coker Tire
1317 Chestnut Street
Chattanooga, TN 37402
(800) 225-7272

These are the tire people. They always have a constant supply of the 185R15 tires with the red stripes. If they don't have the proper tire for your Triumph restoration you're in trouble.

Cox and Buckles
Market Road
Richmon, Surrey
England

This is one of the best Triumph stores in the world. They're also associated with Moss Motors. If you're restoring a Triumph in the United States and can't locate that rare part try these people. If they can't locate the part start worrying.

Eastwood Company
580 Lancaster Ave.
Malvern, PA 19355
(800) 345-1178

This company was founded by an English sports car addict. He doesn't stock any Triumph items. What he does carry is the most complete line of restoration products in the world. If you intend to do anything to your Triumph get this catalog. Eastwood is one stop shopping for restoration supplies.

Eight Parts
4060 Michigan
Tucson, AZ
(602) 748-8115

This group specializes in eight-cylinder Triumph parts. That makes them even rarer than the eight-cylinder Triumphs. If you have a TR8, or Stag, you should get to know these people.

Hart Racing Services
73-76 Britannia Road
London, SW6
England

This firm does a great deal of Stag work. They even created the only Stag racer in the world. They also built a Stag pickup truck. The firm obviously believes in Stags.

Moss Motors
P.O. Box MG
Goleta, CA 93116
(800) 235-6954

Moss Motors has every part you could possibly need for your Triumph. They're probably the oldest British parts supplier in the United States. There was a time when they were the only place you could buy parts for your T-Series MG. Now they're probably the largest vintage parts supplier in the world.

Nisonger Instrument Sales and Service
570 Mamaroneck Ave.
Mamaroneck, NY 10543
(914) 381-1952

This is a source for tachometer and gauge rebuilding. They also have a lot of the older gauges for sale. If you need your TR2 gauges repaired then call Nisonger.

Rimmer Bros.
Triumph House
Sleaford Road
Bracebridge Heath
Lincolnshire LN4 2NA
England

I've met Stag owners who believe this is the finest Stag supplier in the world. They also carry a full range of parts for the complete Triumph line, including the Dolomite Sprint. That's a Triumph most Americans have never even seen.

Roadster Factory
P.O. Box 332
Armagh, PA 15920
(800) 678-8764

This company has done more to change the world of Triumph parts than all the vendors in the world. A fairly new company, they are almost fanatical in their devotion to Triumphs. What started out as a TR3 company now carries parts for everything but the Stags.

Ragtops & Roadsters
213 5th Street
Perkasie, PA 18944
(215) 257-1202

During the past few years Mike Engard has been developing a reputation for building some of the best Triumph restorations in the country. This is a small shop where your car gets personal attention. Mike also caries a lot of old British parts in stock.

Sports & Classics
512 Boston Post Road
Darien, CT 06820
(203) 655-8731

These are the only people I know who have a catalog dedicated to the TR5/TR250, that's how complete they are. If it's a Triumph part you want they have it. They may even have some old factory original items left on the shelf.

S+S Preparations
Oakdene Service Station
Stubbins Lanes, Ramsbottom
Nr. Bury, Lancs BLO OPT
England

These are TR7 and TR8 specialists. They only deal with the final Triumph sports cars. They offer a complete range of service and parts on the final cars.

Southern Triumph Services
11A Stamford Road
Southbourne Bournemouth
England

This one of the oldest Triumph dealers in England. They not only sell parts but they also service the full Triumph range. They're especially strong when it comes to dealing with the forgotten GT6.

The Stag Centre
381/2/3 Geffrye Street
London, England E2

This company started specializing in Stags in 1988. They carry a full range of Stag new and used parts.

TR Bitz
Unit 3, Lyncastle Way
Barley Castle Trading Estate
Appleton, Warrington
Cheshire WA4 4SN
England

This is one of larger, more established Triumph parts suppliers. They specialize in the TR2, 3, 3A, 4, 4A, 5, and 6.

TR Spares
Alpine, CA
(619) 445-8614

Finally someone is making the TR2 and TR3 fender skirts. These are the only people I know that are reproducing these items. The real question is how many Triumph owners will buy them?

Triumph Bookshop
P.O box 28
Market Haraborough
Leicestershire LEI 69SP
England

This is a bookshop that specializes in Triumph books. They carry a complete range for all the owners manuals to workshop manuals. This may be the only place in the world to get some of the books that are no longer in print.

Victoria British Ltd.
Box 14991
Lenexa, KS 66285-4991
(800) 255-0088

I've bought a lot of parts from these people over the years and never had a problem. They know what they're selling and provide you with prompt service. Get a copy of their catalog before you start buying a lot of parts for your garage toys.

TR6 & TR7 Commission Numbers

What the Numbers Mean

Triumph serial numbers are actually very easy to understand. Only in the later models does it get a little difficult, and then because Triumph includes a lot more information in the serial number. The TR2 began with the very simple TS1 and went through to TS8636. All the cars were given consecutive numbers and it couldn't have been easier. The cars between TS1 and TS4002 are called the "long-door" models, with the short-door version beginning at TS4003.

TS8637 through TS13045 encompassed all the TR3 models with Lockheed drum brakes at all four corners. The switch to Girling front disc brakes began with TS13046 and continued through to TS22013. All these cars had small mouth front aprons and the flush mounted grilles.

The wide mouth grille, exterior door handles, and trunk latch began with TS22014, and continued through to TS82346. This was obviously the most popular TR with over 60,000 examples being built.

With the arrival of the TR3B, and TR4, things get a little more confusing. The TR3B was created just in case the TR4 was a massive failure. Thus, the TR3B was a special model. There were two distinct series of TR3Bs.

There was the first group of TR3Bs, TSF1 through TSF830, which were built between March and October of 1962. These cars were identical to the TR3A. Identical until Triumph ran out of parts and substituted different parts. This fact is dealt with in the TR3B chapter.

TCF1 to TCF2804 were built between May and October of 1962 and had the TR4 engine and all-synchro transmission. This meant that during October of 1962 Triumph was actually building three different TR series from the same plant. They were the TR4 and two different TR3Bs.

The TR4 began in August of 1961 and started with serial number CT1. This series continued until January 1965 stopping at commission number CT40304. All very simple.

The TR4A, with IRS, took on a new prefix, CTC. They began producing the TR4A in January 1965 with CTC50001 and ended with CTC78684. The TR4A with the straight axle simply continued the CT numbers. Once again Triumph had a couple of different serial numbers in production at the same time.

The TR250, and TR5, meant another change in prefix numbers. Prior to 1973 all the numbers for carburetor models started with CC. After that date they were prefixed with CF. The following chart provided by The Roadster Factory helps sort out the confusion.

Production Figures and Commission Number References for TR6 Carburetor Models

Model Year	First Number	Production Date	Final Number	Production Date
1969	CC25001	09/68	CC32142	11/69
1970	CC50001	11/69		
1971			CC67893	08/71
1972	CC75001	08/7	1CC85737	08/72
1973	CF1	08/72		08/73
1974	CF12501	09/73		08/74
1975	CF27001	08/74		01/75
1975	CF35001	01/75	CF39991	08/75
1976	CF50001	08/75	CF58328	07/76

CC Prefix - Carburetor Models Built Prior to 1973
CF Prefix - Carburetor Models Built After 1973
L Suffix - Left Hand Drive Models Prior to 1972
U Suffix - Left Hand Drive Models After 1972
O Suffix - Overdrive

Production Figures and Commission Number References for TR6 Fuel Injection Models

Model Year	First Number	Production Date	Final Number	Production Date
1969	CP25001	11/68	CP26998	12/69
1970	CP50001	12/69		
1971			CP54584	09/71
1972	CP75001	09/71	CP77718	09/72
1973	CR1	11/72	CR2911	10/73
1974	CR5001	09/73		
1975			CR6701	01/72

CP Prefix - Fuel Injection Prior to 1973
CR Prefix - Fuel Injection After 1973
L Suffix - Left Hand Drive Model
O Suffix - Overdrive

The trick to understanding all these numbers is to remember that the prefix and suffix letters give you certain information about the cars and the number gives you the production sequence.

TR7 Prefix Codes
When Triumph got to the TR7 they made a change in the prefix by switching to the letter A.
The rest of the prefix is actually an engine code.

Prefix	Model
ACG1	Up to 1977 model year
ACL1U	USA Federal model up to 1977
ACL1UC	USA California model up to 1977
ACW1U	USA Federal model 1977 through 1978
ACW1UC	USA California model 1977 through 1978
ACW1N	Canadian model 1977 through 1979
TCW100,001	USA Coupe, 1979
TCT100,001	USA Convertible, 1979

Vehicle numbering system from 1980 forward

TPVEJ8AT	USA Coupe, Manual Transmission LHS
TPVEJ4AT	USA Coupe, Automatic Transmission LHS
TPZEJ8AT	California Coupe, Manual Transmission LHS
TPZEJ4AT	California Coupe, Automatic Transmission LHS
TPLEJ8AT	Canadian Coupe, Manual Transmission LHS
TPVDJ4AT	Canadian Coupe, Automatic Transmission LHS
TPVDJ8AT	USA Federal Convertible, Manual Transmission LHS
TPVDJ4AT	USA Federal Convertible, Automatic Transmission LHS
TPZDJ4AT	USA California Convertible, Manual Transmission LHS
TPZDJ4AT	USA California Convertible, Automatic Transmission LHS
TPLDJ8AT	Canadian Convertible, Manual Transmission LHS
TPLDJ4AT	Canadian Convertible, Automatic Transmission LHS

Note: The 1980 Model Year Begins at VIN 200001.
The 1981 Model Year begins at VIN 402001

Vehicles built at the Solihull plant begin with VIN 400001, and have the same 8 digit prefix code as shown above except that the eighth letter will be A rather than T.
All TR8 models use the prefix ACN1.
Additional serial number information is available in The Roadster Factory TR7 and TR8 parts catalog. Call (814) 446-4412.

Total TR Production Figures

Model	Years Manufactured	England	Export	Total
TR2	AUG 1953-OCT 1955	2,823	5,805	8,628
TR3	OCT 1955-SEP 1957	1,286	12,091	13,377
TR3A	SEP 1957-OCT 1961	1,896	56,340	58,236
TR3B	MAR 1962-OCT 1962		3,331	3,331
TR4	AUG 1961-JAN 1965	2,592	37,661	40,253
TR4A	JAN 1965-AUG 1967	3,075	25,390	28,465
TR5	OCT 1967-NOV 1968	1,161	1,786	2,947
TR250	AUG 1967-DEC 1968		8,484	8,484
TR6	NOV 1968-JUL 1976	8,370	86,249	94,619
	TOTALS:	21,203	237,137	258,340
	PERCENT:	8%	92%	100%

There are several sets of production figures floating around on the TR series. The problem is that no one seems inclined to go through all 170,000 individual records held by the British Motor Industry Heritage Trust. The other problem is that some people count the Italias, and some people do not. Triumph also supplied kits that could be assembled at a different site. These cars are generally labeled CKD kits. The major point in all this is simply to demonstrate how few Triumphs remained in England. The great numbers questions will continue until all the Triumphs have vanished from the earth.

Spitfire Sales Figures
All Sales Figures by Calendar Year

Year	Spitfire	Sprite	Midget	GT6
1963	6,224	5,343	3,517	
1964	8,761	5,755	4,363	
1965	9,097	5,198	5,561	
1966	6,782	5,379	3,838	
1967	5,643	4,793	3,505	2,000
1968	5,711	4,759	3,556	4,302
1969	6,240	6,255	4,730	4,254
1970	6,305	1,766	10,895	4,066
1971	8,266		10,683	2,970
1972	9,687		12,154	2,753
1973	7,796		11,652	2,198
1974	7,373		8,962	115
1975	8,857		9,048	
1976	6,846		11,219	
1977	9,463		11,892	
1978	10,231		9,385	
1979	8,344		9,165	
1980	4,037		1,902	
1981	3,924		284	
TOTALS:	139,587	39,248	136,311	22,658

TR6 & Spitfire Paint and Trim Codes

TR6

Charles Runyan of The Roadster Factory provided most of the material in this section. The Roadster Factory is a company dedicated to the singular purpose of preserving old Triumphs. They've done an outstanding job at this.

The TR6 used a very basic paint code. The second digit in the paint code gives you the basic color while the first digit gives you the shade of that color.

1 - Black	4 - Yellow	7 - Purple
2 - Red	5 - Green	8 - Grey
3 - Brown	6 - Blue	9 - White

TR6 Paint Codes

Color	Model Year(s)	Code
Shades of Red		
Signal Red	1969-1971	32
Pimento	1972-1976	72
Carmine	1973-1976	82
Magenta	1973-197?	92
Shades of Brown		
Sienna	1971-1973	23
Maple	1974-1975	83
Russet Brown	1976	93
Shades of Yellow		
Jasmine	1969-1972	34
Saffron	1971-1972	54
Mimosa	1973-1975	64
Topaz	1975-197?	84
	1976	94
Shades of Green		
Triumph Racing Green	1969-1970	25
Laurel	1969-1971	55
Emerald	1972-1973	65
1975 BRG	1975-1976	75
Java	1975-1976	85
Shades of Blue		
Royal Blue	1969-1971	56
Sapphire	1972-1974	96
Mallard	1973-1974	106
French Blue	1973-1975	126
Delft	1975-1976	136
Tahiti Blue	1976	146
Shades of Purple		
Damson	1969-1972	17
Shades of White		
White	1969-1976	19

TR6 Trim Colors

Color	Model Year(s)	Code
Black	1969-1976	11
Matador Red	1969-1971	12
Light Tan	1969	13
New Tan	1970-1974	33
Chestnut	1973-1974	63
Beige	1975-1976	74
Shadow Blue	1969-1974	27

Some early TR6s may have had leather interiors, though certainly not very many. An H prefix on the trim code indicates a leather interior.

Spitfire

The Spitfire used the same basic paint codes as the TR6. The second digit in the paint code gives you the basic color while the first digit gives you the shade of that color.

1 - Black	4 - Yellow	7 - Purple
2 - Red	5 - Green	8 - Grey
3 - Brown	6 - Blue	9 - White

Basic Color	1st Shade	2nd Shade	3rd Shade	4th Shade
Black	11 Black			
Red	72 Pimento	82 Carmine		
Brown	83 Maple	93 Russet		
Yellow	64 Mimosa	74 Beige	84 Topaz	194 Inca Yellow
Green	75 BRG	85 Java		
Blue	126 French Blue	136 Delft	146 Meteor Blue	
Purple				
Grey				
White	19 White			

Spitfire Competition Parts

Triumph used the Spitfire as a showcase for its racing ability. They maintained an active competition program throughout the life of the car. Below is a listing of the parts they offered. Take special note of the prices.

V170	Rear Suspension Camber Compensator	$24.95
V175	Competition Four-tube Exhaust System	$67.00
V174	Non-slip Differential, 4.55:1 Ratio	$115.00
V175	"B" Camshaft	$58.75
V176	Competition Valve Springs	$7.80
V177	Oil Radiator Kit	$69.95
V178	Wide (4 1/2") Wheels	$20.70 each
V181	Bendix Electric Fuel Pump	$25.75
V339	Alternate Grille Assembly	$29.95
V340	Koni Competition Front Shocks	$24.00 each
V341	Koni Competition Rear Shocks	$24.00 each
V391	Non-slip Differential 4.11:1	$115.00
V392	Non-slip Differential 4.55:1 (Case Only)	$20.00
V393	Non-slip Differential 4.11:1 (Case Only)	$20.00
V398	Competition Rear Brake Linings	$38.00 set
V400	Competition Front Springs	$15.50
V401	Competition Rear Springs	$40.00
301698	Differential Cage Unit	$15.62
502017	4.87:1 Rear Axle Ratio	$27.87
502017	4.55:1 Rear Axle Ratio	$27.87
508904	Complete Nose Section (4.87:1 Gears)	$142.50
508905	Complete Nose Section (4.55:1 Gears)	$142.50
511401	Overdrive Kit	$287.50
512339	Competition Front Brake Pads	$12.88 set

Index